# THE VICTORIAN GARDEN ALBUM

# THE VICTORIAN GARDEN ALBUM

Compiled by ELIZABETH DRURY
& PHILIPPA LEWIS

PB
PARKGATE
BOOKS

*Frontispiece: 'The Boy's Own Alpine Garden',*
*a chromolithograph from the* Boy's Own Paper.

First published in Great Britain in 1993
by Collins & Brown Limited

Published in 1996 by Parkgate Books
London House, Great Eastern Wharf
Parkgate Road, London, SW11 4NQ



1 3 5 7 9 8 6 4 2

British Library Cataloguing-in-Publication Data:
A catalogue record for this book
is available from the British Library.

ISBN 1 85585 300 0

Conceived, edited and designed by Collins & Brown Limited

Art Director: Roger Bristow
Editor: Colin Ziegler
Designed by: David Fordham

Filmset by Bookworm Typsetting, Manchester
Reproduction by Daylight, Singapore

Printed and bound in Italy by Manfrini S.p.a. Calliano (TN)

# Contents

# INTRODUCTION

THE VICTORIANS were extraordinarily interested in gardening. 'Go where you will in town or country, the love of flowers is displayed on every hand', wrote John R. Mollison. 'It holds sway in the city from the button-hole bouquet to the great floral exhibitions; from the struggling geranium in the city alley to the gorgeous display in the parks and public gardens. In the country it is a poor cottage that has not its flower-plot or window plant.'

The practice of horticulture was regarded as healthy employment and delightful recreation, and in the departments of culinary vegetables and fruits there was the important element of utility. The mid-nineteenth century saw the publication of a great number of books and magazines aimed either at the new generation of gardening enthusiasts or the head gardeners of large establishments in the country. They contained advice – practical, scientific, occasionally whimsical – on every aspect of the subject: the design of a formal parterre, the planting of a window box, floral arrangements for the parlour and dining-room, and how best to rid the garden of weeds and the hothouse of pests. Some books were addressed specifically to ladies; others were written for the enlightenment of children. In the way of amusement as well as education, floral games became popular, as did pressing flowers and simulating them in paper and wax.

# INTRODUCTION

That an understanding of the fundamentals of horticulture was universally beneficial, the Victorians were in no doubt, and the spread of the allotment system from the 1880s served to acknowledge this. The alliance of science and Christianity never, perhaps, seemed more natural than with the publication in 1899 of the fourth issue of *One and All Gardening: A Popular Annual for Amateurs, Allotment-holders and Working-gardeners*; it included articles entitled 'Gardening Helps Body, Mind and Spirit', by the Rev. Canon Barnett, 'The Claims of Gardening on One and All', by Charles Booth (founder of the Salvation Army), and 'Gardening Helps to Cultivate Human Virtues', by His Excellency the Russian Ambassador.

While the boundaries of scientific knowledge (and presumably religious understanding as well) were being extended, so, too, were territorial boundaries. Plants were now sent back to Britain from all over the world and in particular from far-off countries of Queen Victoria's empire; frequently this was done under the auspices of the Royal Horticultural Society. 'The weeds of one country,' remarked Dr Edward Daniel Clarke, 'are the flowers of another'; and to this Samuel Beeton, in *The Book of Garden Management*, added, 'truly a glance at our garden parterres serves to carry us in imagination to many a distant clime. The damask rose . . . grows wild in the sunny plains of Syria. The hollyhock, once known as the "Foreign Rose", and now common in every cottage garden, is of Eastern origin. Fuchsias, which now have their crimson and purple bells in every garden, were brought by enterprising travellers from the depths of untravelled Mexican forests, where, half-hidden beneath their tropical foliage, stand the ruins of vast and richly-sculptured temples and palaces of the Montezumas, where also was found the passion-flower.' The natural climates of some of the more exotic introductions could be simulated under glass, and a range of new structures together with boilers for the production of heat, were designed for this purpose.

# INTRO-DUCTION

The Victorians indulged their fantasies with the creation of different worlds within their gardens. Thus the conservatory or 'stove' (as the glasshouse heated to a high temperature was known) became their tropical jungle; the rockery, their Alpine scene; plantings of rhododendrons, azaleas and magnolias would be named the American Garden and the terraces with fountains and statues called the Italian Garden.

One who had a profound influence on mid-Victorian taste in gardening was Shirley Hibberd, author of many books including *Rustic Adornments for Homes of Taste*. Within it are chapters on the Wardian case, a type of showcase suitable for the indoor display of plants; on floral ornaments for the table and the window; on the aviary and apiary, with comments on their suitability as garden ornaments; on the pleasure garden and flower garden; on the rockery and the fernery; and on garden embellishments such as garden buildings, vases and statuary and the management of a rosary in all seasons. It covered everything on which a gardener in country or town, indoors or out of doors, might wish to be advised.

In addressing the question of how a garden should be planned, Hibberd described the ideal large garden of the mid-nineteenth century: 'It should first of all be laid out so that every diversity of surface may be turned to good account to increase its beauty; the hollows should be made deeper, the elevations higher. Near the house the artificial tone should be highly cultivated, for here at least the garden is but an amplification of the house itself – here, if you can, have a terrace to overlook the brightest scenes you have. Along the southern and west sides of the building, if the garden be on that side, construct a terrace half as high as the house is high. Let this terrace be truly Italian, with balustrades, vases and statuary; with climbing plants of the richest character to scale its most salient angles. From this terrace let a flight of stone steps lead to another terrace, of double

INTRO-
DUCTION

the width of the first, and let this lower terrace be laid out as an elaborate flower garden, on a ground of turf, with stone fountains, statues, vases, and one or two highly-wrought tables and seats of iron or bronze . . . From this lower terrace let your paths lead off over lawns sprinkled with evergreens, flower-beds, avenues of deciduous trees, for which hornbeam, lime, or horse chestnut, would be best . . . From the drawing and dining-rooms you have glass passages, leading to your conservatory, greenhouses, bird and bee-houses; and from one side of the grounds the whole of these houses are visible, and form a noble addition to your home of taste.'

Elsewhere in the book Hibberd insisted on the importance in the garden of foliage plants and of borders of hardy herbaceous plants. This was taken up by William Robinson, who despised the practice of bedding out that left the beds empty for a large part of the year and promoted a natural style of gardening exemplified by the herbaceous border. He inspired admiration for cottage gardens in springtime, which in *The English Flower Garden* he described as 'all ablaze with Primroses of half a dozen colours, Violets, Pansies, Crown Imperials, blue Anemones, purple Aubretia, and white Arabis'.

Reproduced on the following pages are passages from these and other books read by the Victorians with an eager, self-improving interest in the cultivation of flowers, fruit and vegetables. Here, too, are advertisements for glasshouses and composts, and for garden furniture and implements; the catalogues from which they ordered seeds and the brightly coloured packets in which the seeds were supplied; hand-written invoices; book plates; a game played with counters of plant portraits; photographs; cards for Christmas, Valentine's Day and Easter; and the glossy flower scraps that they mounted in scrap albums. No more vivid picture could be created of the practice of horticulture and the Victorians' passion for flowers than with these fragments from the past.

## MARCH

VEGETABLES. – Continue to dig and manure ground for cropping; sow the principal crops of onions and leeks early in the month; from the second week to the end of the month sow the principal crops of broccoli, cauliflowers, carrots, parsnips, parsley, borecole, savoys, brussels sprouts, York, Nonpareil, Enfield Market, and flat Dutch cabbages. Sow once a fortnight marrowfat peas, long pod and Windsor beans, spinage, orange jelly and white Dutch turnips, lettuces, radishes, mustard, and cress; sow in hot-beds celery, cauliflowers, and small salads; plant early potatoes, as well as those intended for the principal crop; also any of those vegetables mentioned last month which may not be finished; plant autumn-sown cabbages, early and late varieties, for principal crops; also herbs, horse radish, cauliflowers, borecole, and brussels sprouts; protect and rod all early peas as they advance.

FLOWERS. – Sow sweet peas, mignonette, lupins, candytufts, virginian stock, and any other very hardy annuals; sow stocks, asters, and other tender annuals in pots or hot-beds; transplant autumn-sown annuals to places where they are intended to flower; prune roses; sow lawn grass seeds for making a new lawn, or on bare patches on the lawn already formed to renovate it; roll lawns, and keep the grass short.

FRUITS. – Complete pruning, training, and transplanting trees and bushes without delay; continue to protect from frost, the flower buds of wall fruit trees as recommended last month; trim strawberry beds, and fork up the soil between the rows, graft apples, pears, plums, and cherries.

## APRIL

VEGETABLES. – Continue to make fortnightly sowings of marrowfat peas, early long-pod and Windsor beans, white and yellow turnips, radishes, lettuces, spinage, curled cress, and white mustard. If not completed last month, sow for the main crop as early as possible leeks, onions, celery, cauliflower, carrots, parsnips, cabbages, and parsley; from the middle to the end of the month sow for the first crop kidney beans, scarlet runners, beet-root, thyme, lavender, sage, and all kinds of herbs. Sow in hot-beds, tomatoes, celery, vegetable marrow, ridge cucumbers, and capsicums. Plant potatoes, cabbages, and cauliflowers for succession. Rod forward peas; earth up the rows of peas, beans, and all kinds of the cabbage tribe; be unremitting in keeping down weeds.

FLOWERS. – Make the principal sowings of showy hardy annuals and biennials; thin out those sown last month as they advance. Sow half-hardy annuals in pots or hot-beds. Plant pansies, carnations, pinks, and hollyhocks. Finish the preparation of beds and borders for bedding plants. Destroy greenfly and caterpillar that may appear on rose bushes. Roll grass lawns frequently, keeping them well mown, and the edges of walks and beds trim and clean.

FRUITS. – Be vigilant in protecting from frost all fruit trees in bloom, exposing the trees in warm sunny weather, shading them if the sun is very strong. Apples and pears may still be grafted early in the month; look to those grafted last month, and see that the clay is still intact. Look after insects, caterpillars, slugs, and other pests, and destroy them as fast as they appear.

## MAY

VEGETABLES. – Sow for succession, as the last sowing appears above ground, marrowfat peas, and Windsor beans, cabbage, lettuce, radish, spinage, turnips, cauliflower, broccoli, mustard, and cress; and for the principal crop, kidney beans, scarlet runners, beet-root, and as early as possible any herbs omitted last month. Towards the end of the month make the first sowing of endive; plant leeks and onions on well-manured soil, also cabbages, lettuces, and cauliflowers for the principal crop; plant tomatoes, against a wall with a southern aspect; thin parsnips if far enough advanced; thin out and weed seed-beds; keep down all weeds; dig and manure ground as it becomes vacant.

FLOWERS. – Sow hardy annuals for succession, and thin out last month's sowings if coming up too thickly; plant out asters, stocks, and other half-hardy annuals. After the second or third week plant out geraniums, calceolarias, lobelia, golden feather, dahlias, and all kinds of summer bedding plants. Stake and tie hollyhocks, carnations, pinks, etc., as they advance; water those in dry weather, and give a little liquid manure. Water anemones and ranunculus. Keep rose-buds and young leaves free of greenfly and caterpillar. Attend to grass lawns and walks.

FRUITS. – Continue protection during frosty nights to any trees still in bloom; water trees recently planted; examine grafts, and see that they are working properly; destroy all insects as far as possible on apricots, cherries, currants, and gooseberries; stir the soil between the rows of strawberries, and give plenty of water in dry weather.

# SPRING

SPRING

JONQUIL

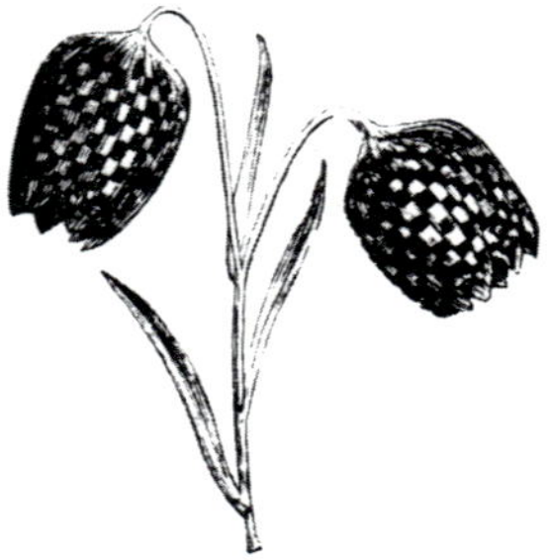

FRITILLARY

# SPRING

MARCH, the dawn of spring, is, in William Howitt's words, 'a rude, and sometimes boisterous month, possessing many of the characteristics of winter; yet awakening sensations perhaps more delicious than the two following spring months, for it gives us the first announcement of spring.'

Trees and shrubs break into bud and leaf, and the earth is bright with early bulbs. Hardly have the crocuses departed before hyacinths make their appearance, blue and single in their wild state, though florists' flowers are double as well, and in white and all shades of red and blue. Following the hyacinth comes the beautiful family of narcissus and the primrose, in its natural form one of the most-loved flowers of spring.

'At this season gardens are becoming interesting to their possessors; and as you walk along past cottages and country-houses, you see the inhabitants astir within them, turning over the fresh yellow mould, planting and sowing for the coming year. All is activity and hope. Look into the cottage garden through the old mossy pales, and see how gay are the little sunny flowers already. There are clumps of dog-tooth violets, rows of yellow daffodils, polyanthuses, and those pretty lilac primroses which only seem to flourish in the gardens of the poor.' So ran the description of the month of March in Mary Howitt's *Calendar of the Seasons*.

SPRING FLOWERS

In March and April several varieties of the densely growing daisy showed their flowers:

*A gold and silver cup*
*Upon a pillar green,*
*Earth holds her Daisy up*
*To catch the sunshine in:–*
*A dial chaste, set there*
*To show each radiant hour;*
*A field-astronomer';*
*A sun-observing flower.*

Henry Sutton

'The month of April', wrote Howitt, 'is proverbial for its fickleness, for its intermingling showers, and fitting gleams of sunshine; for all species of

Narcissus

weather in one day; for a wild mixture of clear and cloudy skies, greenness and nakedness, flying hail and abounding blossoms.' The early cherry, plum and pear trees are by now nearly out of blossom and have their fruit set; the apple blossom is in full perfection.

'Few neglect the culture of those sweet flowers', wrote David Thomson of the wallflower in his *Handy Book of the Flower-Garden*; 'a nook should always be devoted to them in the flower-garden, where ladies and gentlemen can conveniently pick a few fresh blooms when they feel disposed'. He commended the wallflower as both effective to the eye and most pleasing to the sense of smell. 'We have seen cottagers strike the double varieties in large flower-pots filled half full of road grit and soil mixed together, placing the pot in a shady window or other place, and covering its mouth sometimes with a pane of glass.'

During May 'the number of plants increases daily', wrote Samuel Beeton. 'Even seeds stored away in dry papers and closely-shut drawers have felt the warm breath of the spirit of life, and are tapping at the prison bars with earnest entreaties. Let us first of all attend to them, and place them where their coiled-up vitality may unwind itself into the perfect structure of vegetable life.' All seeds intended to flower during the summer – sweet peas, clarkias, mignonettes among them, were sown during the month of May.

In gardens where bedding out was practised this was a busy time of year. Seeds sown in September at greenhouse temperature had made strong plants by the end of May. Those propagated by cutting had been sheltered from the cold and damp during winter and they, too, were ready to be picked out into easily moveable frames or boxes. Pelargonium, salvia,

Flower of Portugal

Spring snowflake

verbena, calceolaria and lobelia were now put out during fine weather to harden off. The quick-growing among them were pinched back to prevent straggling growth.

The process of planting out had to be planned with great precision: Samuel Beeton wrote, 'Let all be done according to a well-digested plan, in which the height and distance of every plant and every bed, are previously determined.'

In the kitchen garden – or that part of a small garden set aside for the cultivation of vegetables – peas and runner beans inch their way up and around the sticks that guide their growth. Heads of asparagus push through the soil of their raised beds; lettuces, radishes, mustard and cress, sown earlier in the spring, are ready for serving as salading; and soon the first gooseberries and currants reach the table, the winter store of preserved fruit generally by now in need of replenishment.

Nut: male and female flowers

Garden anemone

# SPRING BULBS

IN THE GARDEN, nothing gave greater pleasure than the appearance of the first of the spring flowers: the snowdrop, crocus, hyacinth, daffodil, tulip and, earliest of all, the winter aconite with its flowers of buttercup gold which were charmingly set in a wheel of green leaves.

*Orders were invited from Howcroft & Watkins for spring bulbs, 'per 100' or 'per Doz.', to be conveyed to the nearest railway station.*

*Place-setting card.*

## Spring Bulbs

*'The hyacinth is the choicest of the whole tribe of welcome spring flowers; its exquisite beauty and delicate perfume make it the very emblem of cheerfulness and promise.'*
Shirley Hibberd

In 'border culture' the bulbs were planted in beds in the autumn and lifted after they had flowered to be dried and stored for another year. William Robinson, in *The Wild Garden*, derided this practice. 'Garden adornment with early bulbs is merely in its infancy,' he wrote in 1870, 'at present we merely place a few of the showiest in geometrical lines,' but he continued, 'cushioned among the grass, the flowers would unfold prettier than they can in the regulation sticky earth of the border.' And so the fashion grew for planting the bulbs in rough grass at the margin of the garden, leaving the plants to die back naturally, the grass to grow till fit to be cut for hay and the bulbs to multiply undisturbed.

*Give-away gardening advice.*

# GARDEN IMPLEMENTS

*Victorian gardeners with the tools of their trade.*

*The bill is from a Staffordshire manufacturer to an ironmonger.*

Wedges Mills, Cannock
STAFFORD
Messrs H. B. Plowright & S
Bought of William
One third of price charged all
TWO THIRDS ONLY FOR THOSE R
Empties, Parcels &c. Addressed to

2 doz CS Garden Hoes ea 4 5 6 in — 1 4 0
1 doz CS Do ea 7 8 9 in — 3 6
1/2 doz CS Dutch Do 3 1/2 in — 2 17 6
1/2 doz CS Imp'd Brit Hay Forks 1 24 15% — 2 8 10 1/2
10 doz CS Bright Norfolk Hoes 6/6 — 3 5 0
2 doz CS Do ea 7 8 in Bury necks — 1 12 0
4 doz CS Do — 1 12 0
Basket 2/9 Bdle Wrapp'd 3d — 3 0
£ 9 12 3
Peterboro

Pickfork.

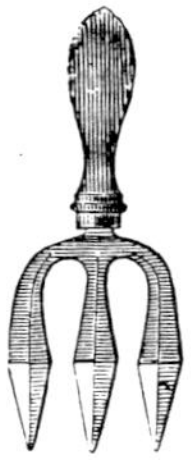

Tan-fork.

# Garden Implements

Gardening implements 'should be kept under cover in an open airy shed or tool house', wrote J. C. Loudon in *The Horticulturist*; 'some, as the spade, pick, &c., may rest on the ground; others, as the scythe, rake, &c., should be suspended on hooks or pins; and smaller articles, such as trowels, dibbers, &c., placed in a holster rail.'

An essential tool was the spade, which could be employed in many different modes of 'stirring the soil'. Robert Thompson, in *The Gardener's Assistant*, expressed his approval of the new steel-faced spades – considerably sharper than the 'dull-working' kinds formerly in use. Steel forks he found light to use and the prongs helpfully 'elastic'.

Cutting instruments, particularly, needed to be cleaned thoroughly before they were put away. The blades of scythes and hedgebills should, according to Loudon, be heated gently before a fire, then 'coated over with grease or bees-wax, and powdered over with lime or chalk to prevent the grease being eaten off by mice'. In well-ordered establishments it was agreed between the master and his men that fines should be imposed on 'all who do not return the tools to their proper places in due time, and properly cleaned.'

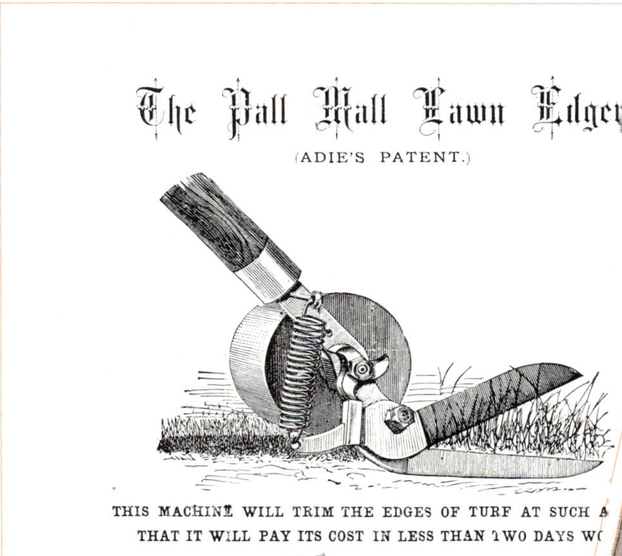

# SEEDS AND CATALOGUES

*Radish seed should be sown before May, according to Cobbett, or it becomes 'hot and disagreeable'.*

VICTORIAN seed catalogues frequently prefaced their listings with advice to their customers such as, 'When winter lingers in the lap of spring each must observe for himself the temperature of the atmosphere and the conditions of the soil and act accordingly.'

In 1889 the Dublin seed merchant W. Tait & Co. presented in his *Select Annual List* no less than forty-six varieties of pea, including American Wonder, 'a very early wrinkled variety', Hundredfold and Telephone, both 'very robust in habit, bearing

*The Queen and her Consort apparently gave the royal approval to Mr Cannell's seeds.*

*'George Wood Ingram presents his concise seed catalogue for 1902, and thanks his Customers for their support in the past season.'*

*An American seed packet.*

immense pods, containing in each ten to twelve peas of exquisite flavour, invaluable for exhibition'. Other vegetables offered were rampion, salsify, cardoon, borecole, eggplant and capsicum.

New for that year was the Prince Albert Victor melon, an ornamental Chilian beet with bronze foliage and a striped Japanese poppy, The Mikado. 'All Orders for Flower Seeds sent Post Free . . . Quality the True Test of Cheapness.'

*'Persons at a distance, who may be unknown to us, will oblige by giving a reference, or accompanying their order with a remittance', declared Young, Oakenhead & Co.*

# NURSERYMEN AND SEEDSMEN

*A description of how the 'seed-room' should be organized is given by Robert Thompson: 'It should contain a cabinet fitted up with drawers for seeds; an airy open case, with drawers for bulbs; shelves for catalogues, a book case, partitioned off, because moths are apt to be introduced along with some kinds of seeds, for the garden library, unless this is kept in the head-gardener's house as part of his furniture.'*

*A trade card for a seedsman from Chicago.*

*J. Lewis & Son's invoice of £4 10s for seven roses and Walter Purvis Hume's of 2/- for two silver birches. C. Hale Jessop offered peaches, figs and vines in pots for hothouses.*

*Many nurseries offered a service in landscape gardening and in keeping gardens 'laid out and kept in order by the day, month or year'.*

## Nurserymen and Seedsmen

Nurserymen and seedsmen doubtless took great delight in cultivating new varieties of plants and in displaying the results of their skill to gardeners and garden owners in their catalogues.

Charles Dudley Warner, who wrote a book with the title *My Summer in a Garden*, described the riches and temptations of a nurseryman's catalogue: 'The things I may do in my garden multiply on my vision . . . Can I raise all those beautiful varieties, each one of which is preferable to the other? Shall I try all the kinds of grapes, and all the sorts of pears? I have already fifteen varieties of strawberries; and I have no idea if I have hit on the right one . . . Oh for the good old days when a strawberry was a strawberry, and there was no perplexity about it! There are more berries now than churches; and no one knows what to believe! The fashions of ladies' bonnets are nothing to the fashion of nurserymen.' Putting an end to his bewilderment, Warner wrote, 'May Heaven keep me to the old roots and herbs of my forefathers! Perhaps, in the world of modern reforms, this is not possible; but I intend now to cultivate only the standard things, and learn to talk knowingly of the rest.'

Among the most famous of the Victorian nurserymen were William Paul of A. Paul & Son of Waltham Cross, Thomas Rivers of Sawbridgeworth, Joseph Cheal of Kent and Thomas Rochford of North London. Each tended to have his own speciality, Rochford was a supplier of palms and Rivers was known for his fruit trees. They promoted their new varieties with letters to gardening magazines and by writing books. W. Tait of Dublin, like many nurserymen, advertised an employment exchange for gardeners: 'Having so extensive a business connection in this country, as well as in England and Scotland, W. Tait & Co. are always in a position to recommend men of first-class ability, experience and character . . . gentlemen can consult our Register at any time.'

*George Watts & Sons, as well as being nurserymen and seedsmen, offered their services as florists and landscape gardeners.*

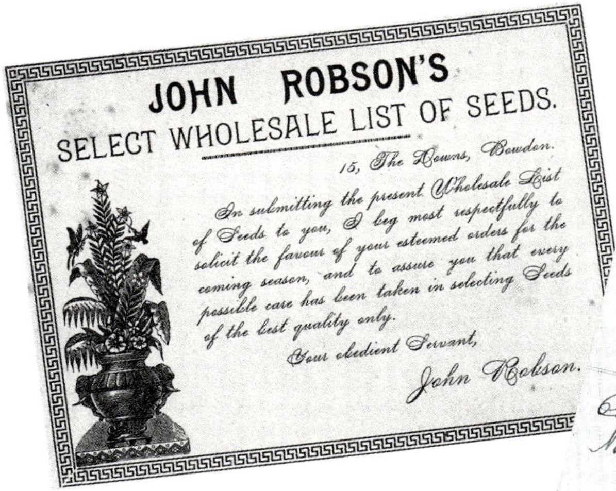

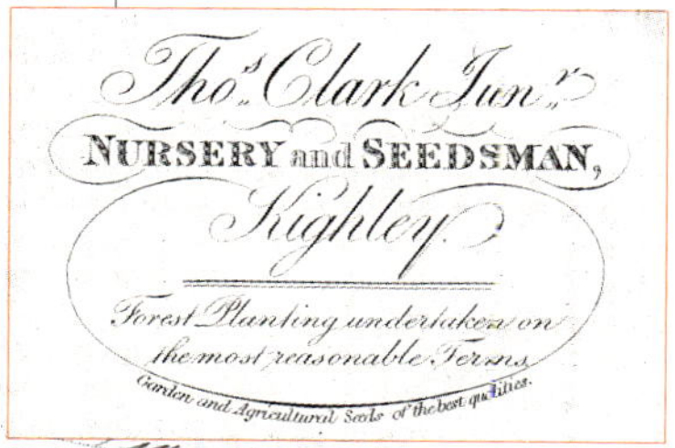

# Flowers for the Spring

*The lily of the valley was defined in the* Dictionary of Gardening *as 'essentially a subject for providing cut flowers and in great demand for bouquets of every description'.*

*'When grown on a well-exposed bank, a patch of violets in full blossom make a magnificent display', wrote Alfred Smee.*

So easy was the cultivation of spring flowers that they were regarded as peculiarly 'the flowers for the million'. To appear in March, April and May the plants were of necessity hardy and 'within the reach of the humblest amateur who commands a few square yards of a flower border, even if he has not so much as a common garden hand-glass', according to David Thomson's *Handy Book of the Flower-Garden*.

'In Spring the Violet is the choicest of our native flowers', wrote Alfred Smee in *My Garden*. He grew the wild unscented violet and purchased an improved florist's variety from Parker of Tooting. Primroses, he noted, attained their greatest perfection in woodland after the undergrowth had been cut back. 'Polyanthus, which is a florist's flower of great merit, should also be grown by hundreds.'

Especially prized was the laced polyanthus, 'the ground colour being dark crimson, maroon, or black, and the lacing consisting of regular marginal bands of various shades of yellow and orange', according to Shirley Hibberd. The giant polyanthus was the showiest by far for the border or flower bed, 'being of all colours, and in many cases extremely beautiful'.

## FLOWERS FOR THE SPRING

*Primula, a plate from* The New Practical Window Gardener, *one of the species described by the author: 'nothing looks better on a balcony than some hardy common flowers which may be bought in the market for a few pence per dozen'.*

# Glass and Glasshouses

Conservatory erected at Alresford, Hants.

Glazed porch, no. 3.

Span-roof forcing house.

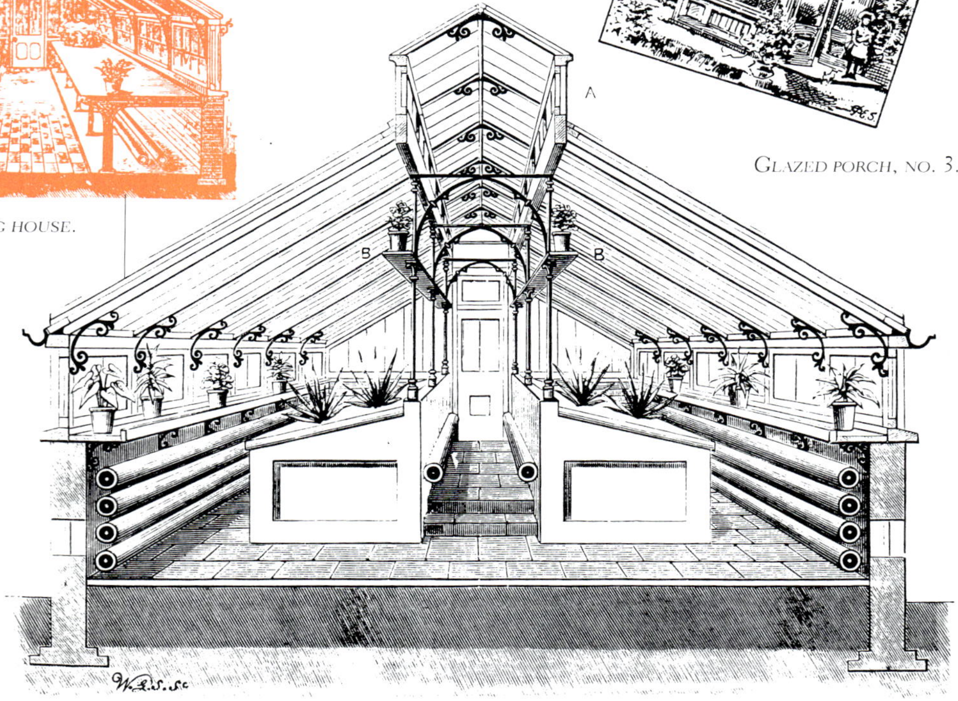


Span-roof pine stove.

Lofty palm houses, stove houses for orchids and any other exotics, ferneries and vineries, greenhouses and elegant conservatories, cucumber frames and cloches: the common component was glass.

In 1845 the tax on glass was abolished. 'Glass structures of even the smallest kind would, a few years ago, have been considered a piece of great extravagance for any but the affluent', wrote Mr Beeton; in the new times of cheap glass 'there is no reason why every house, suburban or country should not have its glass house proportioned to its size; and we shall be able to show that an additional rent of 7½% would amply repay any landlord the necessary outlay.'

By the middle of the century, firms such as Boulton & Paul of Norwich were offering for sale a range of glasses that included a peach house, a glazed porch (with wooden foundations, removeable on the expiration of the lease of a house), a 'portable universal plant preserver' and a 'wall fruit-tree protector'. Much advice was available on the angle at which glass should be placed to achieve the best results, and there was also an abundance of information on ventilation, fumigation and the comparative advantages of heating the glasshouse by hot water pipes, steam or hot air.

ROSE LANE WORKS NORWICH 13

**CONSERVATORY AND PALM HOUSES.**

**CONSERVATORY.**

Erected for T. Pim, Esq., Bexley Heath, Kent.

Connected with this Conservatory is a very fine Range of Three-Quarter Span Houses, comprising Fernery, Vineries, and Peach Houses, 250 ft. in length.

*Glasshouses from the catalogue of Boulton & Paul, Manufacturers, Rose Lane Works, Norwich, April, 1895.*

## GLASS AND GLASSHOUSES

# Town Gardens

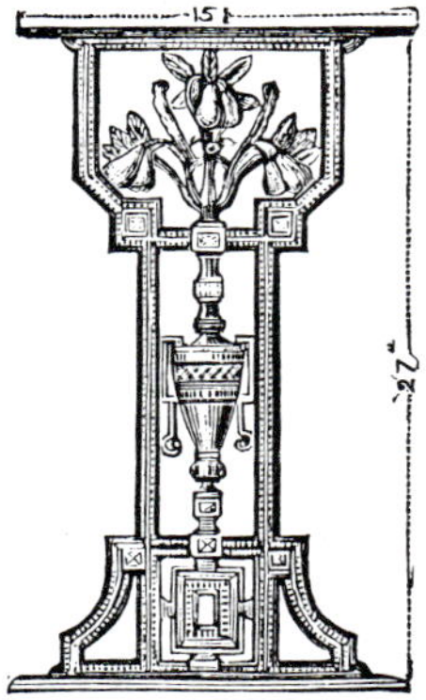

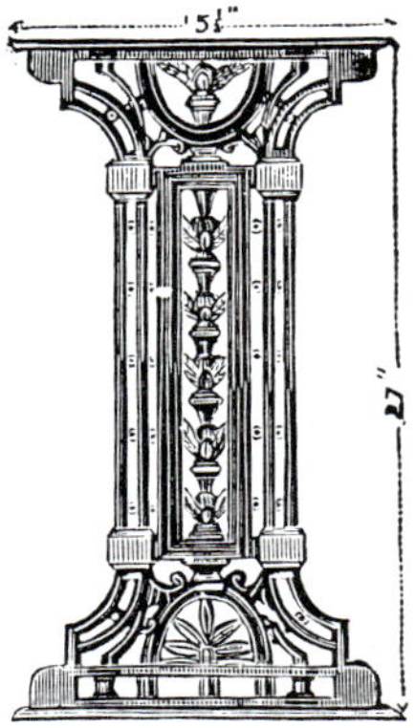

A new breed of gardener came into being during the reign of Queen Victoria as a large part of the population moved from the country into the towns. The wealthier among them lived in suburban villas that took land from the surrounding fields. It was for these 'bank clerks, thrifty traders, agents, actuaries and poor authors', that the weekly *Amateur Gardening* was published, and W. S. Rogers wrote *Villa Gardens* and Shirley Hibberd *The Town House: A Manual for the Management of City and Suburban Gardens*. Hibberd's hope was that those 'in populous cities pent would assemble round their homes as much floral beauty as the circumstances of the case would admit,' and his book was full of straightforward, practical advice.

For the front garden he recommended gravel, first-rate evergreens,

*Rockeries were originally felt to be the correct habitat for the gnome. Gnomes were first introduced by Sir Charles Isham in his rockery at Lamport Hall. The iron table stands (far left) are from the catalogue of O'Brien, Thomas and Company.*

*Illustration from the German catalogue of Heisner gnomes: 'Imagine your customer's delight in possessing such artistic ornaments.'*

flower beds and a screen of chestnut or lime trees to enable the owner to enjoy 'a patrician breadth of leafiness and blossom undisturbed by the traffic of the highway'. Kitchen plots, he wrote, should always be distinct from the flower garden as it was in the poorest taste to have to walk past rows of cabbages to reach shady arbours and the beds of roses.

Hibberd offered the achievement of a 'world of perennial loveliness beyond the influence of our commercial hurry'.

# Horticultural Skills

*Budding was the usual method of propagating the standard rose, using wild dog rose as the stock. These engravings show two stages of the grafting process (right and opposite above).*

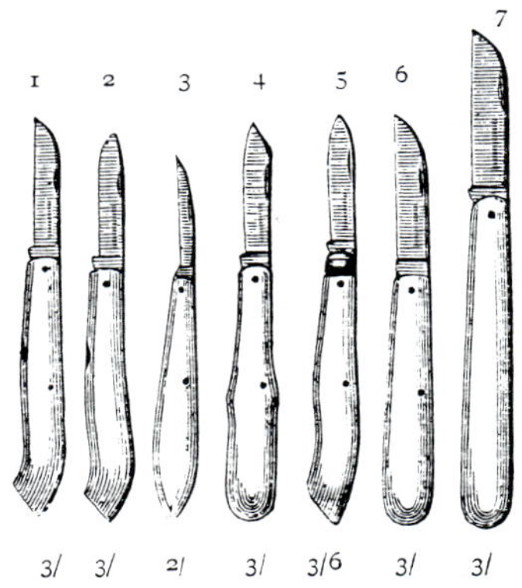


**BUDDING KNIVES with Ivory Handles.**

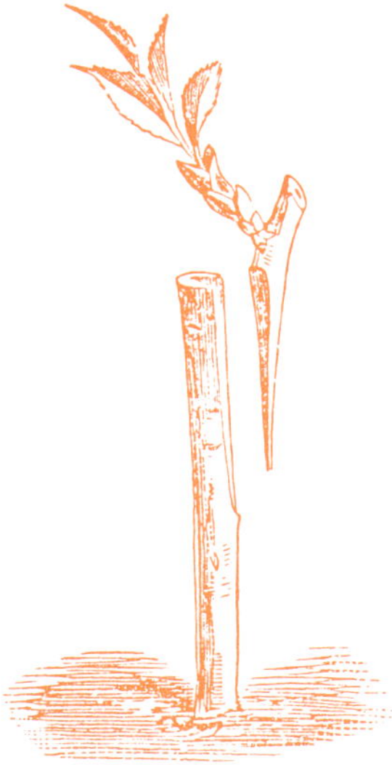

PROPAGATING, pruning and training were three of the skills of the Victorian gardener. Books for the amateur and the professional gardener provided clear instructions on how the operations should be performed; illustrations of the delightful effects produced by training encouraged enterprise.

Budding, one of the methods of propagating by division, required 'the greatest nicety and exactness', as described by Mrs Loudon in *Gardening for Ladies*. Using a budding knife (thin and ivory handled), a young shoot – of the rose or pear, for instance – was inserted under the bark of another plant and tightly bound until the bud had united with the parent tree; this, apart from the stem and roots, was afterwards cut away.

The process of propagating most commonly employed for fruit trees, and for flowering shrubs such as the camellia, was grafting. A Monsieur Noisette in France had enumerated a hundred and thirty-seven methods for carrying out the union of the scion (the shoot of the plant to be propagated) with the stock (the established plant). The process of inarching was also known as 'grafting by approach'. The scion remained attached to the parent tree until the union had been effected.

Fig. 249.

Horizontal Training with a Double Stem.

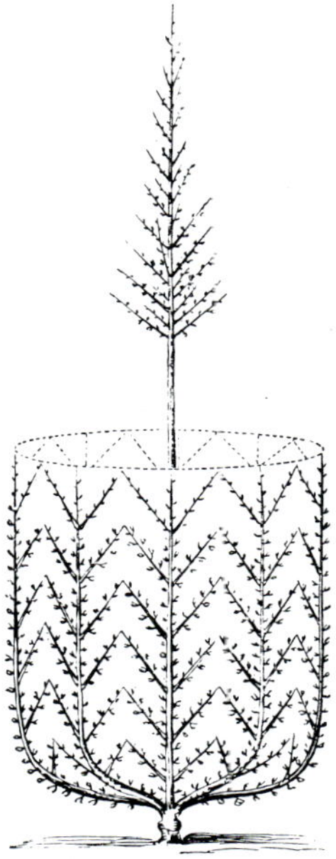

Vase Pyramid.

# HORTI-CULTURAL SKILLS

'To train a plant,' in the words of Mr Loudon, 'is to support or conduct its stem and branches in some form or position, either natural or artificial, for purposes of use or ornament.' Pears were trained in pyramids, rose trees in balloons, laburnums in arches. In *The Horticulturist* Loudon noted that woollen shreds were preferred to any other material for holding the branches in shape as they were softer and 'less influenced by the weather'.

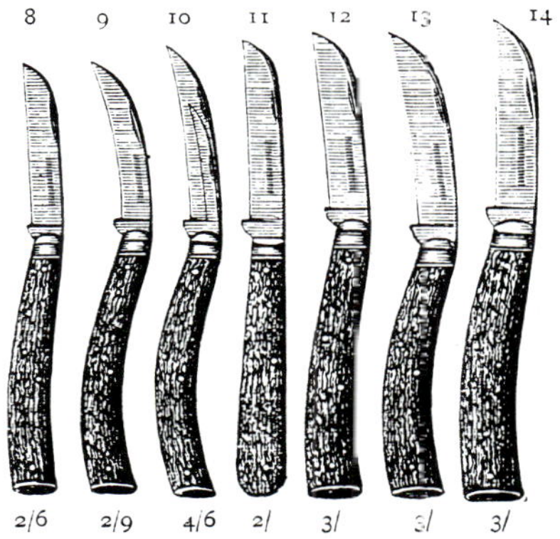


**PRUNING KNIVES with Stag Handles.**

*The rough surface of the horn handles was designed to prevent the hand from slipping.*

*The 'plain house' or cottage has grape vines on the left of the front door and fruit trees on the right.*

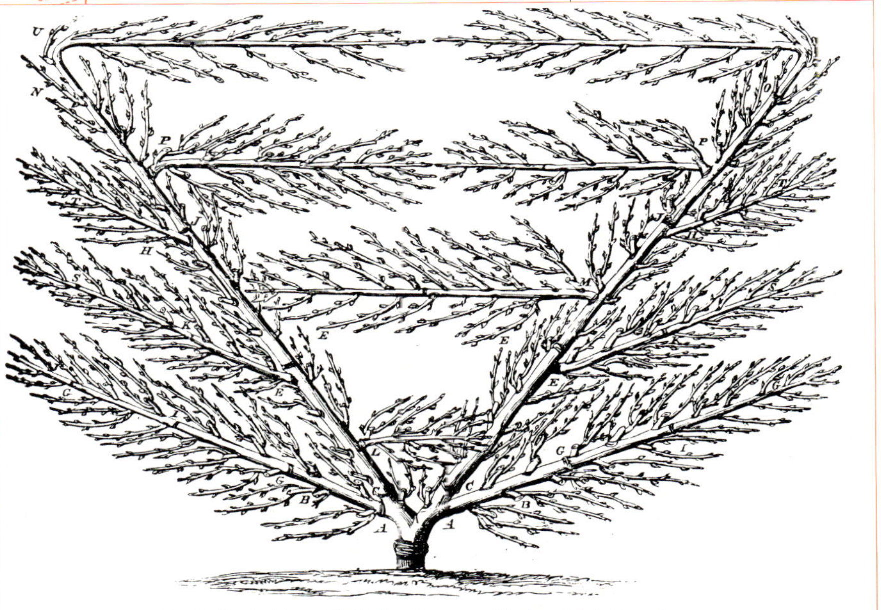

Peach—Fan-training, with the branches reversed horizontally in the centre.

# The Poultry Yard

*Cups, bound volumes and even cash were offered as prizes for winning pouter pigeons, game bantams and brahma hens.*

The desirability of every household being provided with eggs and the occasional duck or goose for the table meant that many gardens, in towns as well as in the country, had a poultry yard. Jane Loudon wrote in *The Country Lady's Companion, or How to Enjoy a Country Life Rationally* that the yard should have a pond for ducks, a roosting tree for guinea fowl and a feeding-house with boilers for cooking their food. Hen houses should be placed against the wall of a chimney, the warmth encouraging the hens to extend their period of laying. The duties of attending on poultry, she commented, are 'completely feminine'. Fancy fowl — silkies, bantams and frizzles — would be kept for their fine looks and for competition.

*The poster stamps were issued by the weekly,* The Smallholder.

# THE POULTRY YARD

*For fattening poultry for the table, steamed potatoes, treacle and malt were recommended, and, for those without regard for economy, 'Ground or pounded rice, scalded with milk and sweetened with sugar . . . Their drink must be beer.'*

*In 'The Art of Housekeeping' it was claimed that even in a London garden chickens paid for themselves in eggs in three months.*

# THE GARDENERS

*'To all the gardeners, whether they serve or rule,' was Dean Hole's dedication in* A Book about the Garden and the Gardener.

MR OLDACRE was handsome and hale, six feet high, 'and straight as a Guardsman, though he has seen the chestnut trees of his great avenue in flower for seventy springs': this was how Dean Hole described a fellow member of his garden society in *A Book about the Garden and the Gardener*. 'Was ever neckerchief so snowy white? Was ever face so bright, so smooth, so roseate? There is a perpetual smile and sunshine in them, and in his clear blue eyes, as though he had lived always among things beautiful, and their exceeding loveliness had made his heart glad. What pyramids of pineapples, what tons of grapes and figs and peaches, what acres of flowers, tender and hardy, those hands have tended.'

A gardener such as Mr Oldacre would be provided with a house by his employer, and 'he should possess it as his castle for the time being', wrote Mr Loudon in *The Horticulturist*. The living quarters of the under-gardeners were generally included in the sheds behind the different plant structures 'because they tend to keep the latter warm, and because the high back wall of the hothouses existing at any rate, they can be erected there much more economically than anywhere else'.

The gardener who grew flowers and vegetables not for his master but on his own account might be a man who had 'run the round of pleasure and business, eaten dirt, and sown wild-oats', as described by Charles Dudley Warner in *My Summer in a Garden*. 'To own a bit of ground, to scratch it with a hoe, to plant seeds and watch their renewal of life, – this is the commonest delight of the race, the most satisfactory thing that a man can do.'

*These gardeners worked for wages ranging from 2/10½d to 1/- per day.*

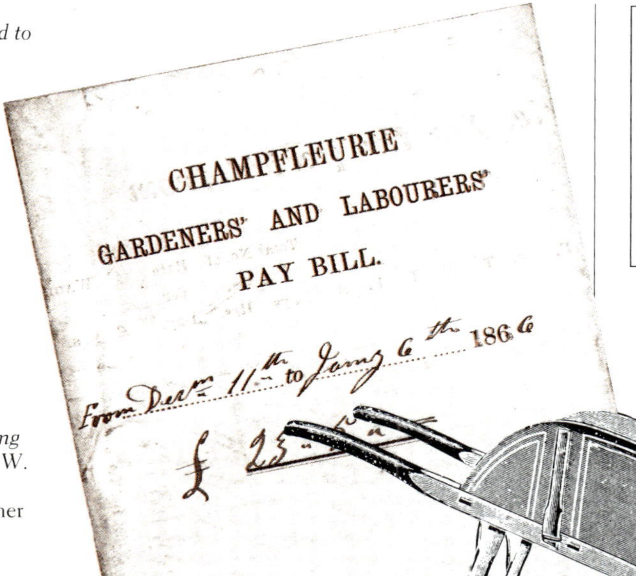
CHAMPFLEURIE
GARDENERS' AND LABOURERS'
PAY BILL.
From Decr 11th to Jany 6th 1866

## THE GARDENERS

*Tom Thumb dahlias growing in beds, with the raiser, T. W. Girdlestone, Esq.; an engraving from* My Gardener *by H. W. Ward.*

THE ST HELIERS GARDEN WHEELBARROW

# Easter Flowers

*The lily of the valley, a native wild flower, was often cultivated in pots for early spring flowering.*

All that was bright and cheerful in the garden, and in the woods and fields, was brought to the church on Easter eve. At Cae Mawr in Wales, in the year 1870, 'Mrs Morrell had been very busy all the morning preparing decorations for the Font, a round dish full of flowers in water and just big enough to fit into the Font and upon this large dish a pot filled and covered with flowers all wild, primroses, violets, wood anemones, wood sorrel, periwinkles, oxlips and the first blue bells, rising in a gentle pyramid, ferns and larch sprays drooping over the brim.' In the churchyard, as described in the Rev. Francis Kilvert's diary entry for the day, children came with baskets of flowers for dressing the graves.

Lilies of all kinds played their part in the Easter celebrations. 'The foliage and flowers of the chaste Trumpet-lily are unsurpassed for the altar and last a considerable time', wrote F. W. Burbidge in *Domestic Floriculture*. 'A good specimen of this plant, or two or three small ones placed together, look remarkably well along with statuary or architectural details.' The white arum lily was another favourite.

A symbol of Easter was the passion flower, said to have been given its name by missionaries.

*All beauteous flower, whose centre*
*glows*
*With studs of gold;*

The column of the ovary bore a fancied resemblance to the cross, the five anthers to the five wounds of Christ, the three stigmas to the three nails, the filaments within the flower to the crown of thorns. The flower stayed open for three days, which was meant to symbolize the three-year ministry of Christ.

# EASTER FLOWERS

*The passion flower; a Victorian scrap.*

*Daffodils and lilies; two cards for Easter.*

# The Rock Garden

'Remote from the house,' Shirley Hibberd wrote in *The Town House*, 'you may throw up some rock-work, and on one side a mound, to be covered with ivy and surmounted by a good-sized shrub. The outside of the rock-work should be built up tastefully with large clinkers, and covered with any large dark masses of rock'. To this he added, 'Do not on any account, stick shells or plaster-casts about your rock-work, the moment you do anything of the kind it becomes childish.'

For those with means, the creation of a rock garden was made somewhat easier in the second half of the nineteenth century with the development by James Pulham of a completely new type of cement. Pulhamite, as it was called, could be poured over piles of clinker, stone or rubble and then modelled so that it took on the appearance of the local rock. Supremely naturalistic effects could be achieved with Pulhamite.

*'Rockwork and common bracken'; Shirley Hibberd's own outdoor fernery, described by him as a 'ruined bastion'.*

*Two groupings of artificial rock from Victorian gardens.*

# THE ROCK GARDEN

*A coloured print, given away with the* Boy's Own Paper, *'Rockery plants and how to grow them', painted expressly for the* Boy's Own Paper *by John Allen Esq.*

*A group of scolopendriums on rockwork.*

With the publication of William Robinson's *Alpine Flowers for English Gardens* came greater knowledge of the plants that were appropriate to a rock garden and how they grew in their natural Alpine habitat: arabis and aubretia had to be sown or planted in the roughest manner to flourish, for instance, while other plants needed different treatment. 'It would be in good taste,' he wrote, 'to have some graceful, tapering young pines planted near, as this type of vegetation is usually to be seen on mountains.' To begin with, these should 'be confined to a few square yards of earth, with no protuberance more than a yard high'.

## JUNE

**VEGETABLES.** – Sow marrowfat peas in the beginning of the month, falling back on earlier sorts to sow for succession. Sow beans, kidney beans, scarlet runners, whitestone and orange-jelly turnips; endive for the principal crop; spinage, lettuce, radish, mustard, and cress for succession. Pinch off the tops of beans coming into flower, so as to swell the pods; hoe and stir the soil between growing crops; and keep down all weeds, removing them at once. Tomatoes may still be planted; keep any that are advanced securely staked or tied.

**FLOWERS.** – Finish planting bedding-plants without delay; peg down young shoots of verbenas and other plants requiring similar treatment; stake hollyhocks, dahlias, carnations, etc., likely to suffer from winds. Take up all autumn-planted bulbs as the leaves decay; clean and store them in a dry cool place. Sow Brompton, East Lothian, and intermediate stocks, and hardy annuals for successional bloom. Mow and roll grass lawns frequently; remove all weeds, and keep everything neat and trim.

**FRUITS.** – Pinch the young shoots of all wall fruit trees not required for the formation of the tree; nail and train those that are required. Pinch or thin out shoots of currants, gooseberries, etc. Clear away young suckers or other superfluous shoots that may be growing from the roots of trees. Spread clean straw or hay between the rows of strawberries as they get ripe, to prevent them being splashed with mud in showery weather. Protect the fruit with nets from small birds; also cherries, and other ripening fruits.

## JULY

**VEGETABLES.** – Plant successional crops of lettuce, cauliflower, celery, parsley, endive, early and late broccoli, borecole, and cabbages. Prick out or plant seedlings of herbs far enough advanced; give all the plants a good soaking of water in the evening. Sow for succession spinage, white, yellow, and Swedish turnips, endive, lettuce, winter-radish, early horn carrot, and cabbage. Be unremitting in keeping down all weeds; clear the ground of exhausted crops, manuring and digging it for immediate cropping. Stake peas and scarlet runners. Take up garlic, shallots, and onions; tie them in bunches, and hang in a dry airy place. Cut and dry herbs.

**FLOWERS.** – Give careful attention to the pegging down and staking of plants requiring such treatment; fill up any vacancies that may occur in flower beds; or, where an isolated sickly plant appears, remove it at once, filling its place with one strong and healthy. Give plenty of water in dry weather – not a mere wetting of the surface, but a thorough drenching. Water bedding plants with liquid manure occasionally. Propagate carnations, picotees, and pinks by layers; pansies and dahlias by cuttings; bud roses, and clear away unsightly decaying blooms. Attend to mowing and rolling grass, and keep all edgings and walks tidy.

**FRUITS.** – Lose no time in pinching or re-pinching all young shoots not permanently required on fruit trees. Collect the strongest runners of strawberries, and plant them in small beds. Loosen the ties of grafts; re-tie them, and secure the young shoots to sticks to protect them from strong winds. Protect ripening fruit from birds.

## AUGUST

**VEGETABLES.** – Sow for the principal crop (to be transplanted in October and in spring). York, Nonpareil, Enfield Market, and Drumhead cabbages; also a little Red Dutch for pickling. Sow endive, winter lettuce, prickly spinage, radish, and small salads, also white Spanish onions for salads. Earth up celery and other advancing crops. Keep stirring the hoe between all growing crops; water copiously in dry weather, and give a little liquid manure occasionally. Remove all ripened crops; trench, manure and dig the ground for future cropping. Continue to take up and dry garlic, shallots, and onions, as they ripen.

**FLOWERS.** – Sow Brompton, East Lothian, and intermediate stocks and hardy annuals for spring flowering. Put cuttings of all the principal varieties of bedding plants into boxes or pans for next year's supply (see that the bottoms of the boxes are properly perforated to allow for thorough drainage); also cuttings of herbaceous plants, such as phloxes, pentstemons, hollyhocks, etc. See that all tall-growing plants are properly staked and tied; give plenty of water in dry weather, and a little liquid manure to plants that may appear sickly, or weak in growth or vigour. Finish budding roses; and remove all decayed leaves and blooms from flower beds; hoe, rake, and roll walks; and let cleanliness and neatness be the order of the day.

**FRUITS.** – Finish pinching in or summer-pruning all young shoots of fruit trees; attend to grafts as last month. Plant the strongest runners of strawberries in ground previously well dug and heavily manured; clear the old beds of weeds and runners.

# SUMMER

SUMMER

GLADIOLUS

# SUMMER

JUNE IS the true beginning of summer. 'The flower-garden' wrote William Howitt, 'is in the height of its splendour. Roses of almost innumerable species – I have counted no less than fourteen in a cottage garden, – lilies, jasmins, speedwells, rockets, stocks, lupines, geraniums, pinks, poppies, valerians, red and blue, mignonettes, etc. and the glowing rhododendron abound. It is the very carnival of Nature. Families of young birds are abroad, and give their

WHITE PINK

SUMMER FLOWERS

parents a busy life of it till they can peck for themselves. Rooks have deserted the rookery, and are feeding their vociferous young in every pasture, and under every garden tree. The swallow and swift are careering in the clear skies.'

*Now broad carnations, and gay*
*spotted pinks,*
*And showered from every bush, the*
*damask rose,*
*Infinite in numbers, delicacies,*
*scents,*
*With hues on hues, expression cannot*
*paint!*

quoted Samuel Beeton in his description of June, 'the leafy month of roses'. Where roses were once grown

VARIEGATED PINK

by the dozen they were now grown by the thousand, and where by the thousand now by the acre.

For Rider Haggard, the garden looked at its most beautiful in the dying hour of a day in early July. 'Now the hush of the night is a thing that may be felt – it is so deep. No leaf stirs upon the trees, no bird sings. The bats flitter and wheel, the moths fade past, the belated bumblebee, or it may be a beetle, drones its way homewards. Out yonder over the lawn appears and disappears a white and ghostly shape, that of a hawking owl. This is all: the rest is sleep and silence; while above, in the blue, the planets spring out singly. Now darkness comes, and the tall many-coloured rods of the Foxglove gather one hue of grey; the golden Iris flowers gleam like fallen stars about the borders, and the gloom is heavy with the odour of Verbena, of Roses, and of the flowering Laurel. It is well to enjoy such nights while one can, for they are few in England.'

Samuel Beeton was enraptured by the early garden fruits, 'now in perfection . . . the black currant hangs like glittering rounded jetty beads beneath its fragrant leaves; the gooseberries can scarcely contain themselves within their hairy husks of green and red; white and red currants hang like pendent pearls and corals

MOSS ROSE

from their broad-leaved boughs, and strawberries, ripe and ready for the banquet, peep from under leaves.'

The beginning of July, in the weeks between the hay and the corn harvests, was the best time for a flower show, in the opinion of Dean Hole. 'It's a little late for plants and a little early for fruit, but good prizes will bring both in abundance.' He portrayed the wearisome life of the competitive gardener in a verse of 'Song of the Exhibitor':

IRIS

*I've been to all the flower shows,*
*north, south, and east, and west,*
*By rails and roads, with huge van*
*loads of plants I love the best;*
*From dusk to dawn, through night to*
*morn, I've dozed 'mid clank and*
*din,*
*And woke with cramp in both my legs,*
*and bristles on my chin,*
*I'm a poor, used up exhibitor,*
*Knocked out of present time*

But after tasting success, he was 'a fine, revived exhibitor'

In August 'The brilliant dahlia, the gorgeous sunflower, and the lordly-looking hollyhock, have taken the place of the lilies', wrote Samuel Beeton. It was the moment of the fragrant mignonette, 'the cherished inhabitant of many a cottage-garden and window-frame'.

*Now summer goes –*
*Lingers, bestows*
*One rich last gift of her making –*
*These, azure-dim,*
*Odorous, slim,*
*Lavender blooms for our taking.*

*So many flowers!*
*Such shining hours!*
*Many a bird's sweet 'Come hither.'*
*Then the rose fades,*
*Hushed are the glades,*
*Lavender's sweet, tho' it wither!*

Agnes Falconer

## SUMMER

FOXGLOVE

# Roses

*'Standard roses may be planted in clumps or in beds on lawns, or along the sides of walks when the borders are filled with plants of low growth.'*

*The Rose Garden, Newtown House, Newbury.*

# Roses

Queen of all Flowers and Empress of all Gardens: this was the sobriquet applied to the rose by that most passionate of Victorian rose growers, Dean Hole.

Extensive breeding during the century widened the choice from the old familiar sweetbriars, scotch, cabbage, monthly, alba and damask roses to include new hybrid species. 'What a diversity, and yet what harmony of colour!' enthused Dean Hole, enumerating roses of white, blush, pink, rose, carmine, crimson, scarlet, vermilion, maroon, purple 'roses almost black, and roses of glowing gold'. But, he avowed, if he were sentenced to possess a single rose tree it would be Gloire de Dijon. A pale apricot hybrid tea, he described it as 'what cricketers call an "all rounder", good in every point for wall, arcade, pillar, standard and dwarf.' Almost equally lauded was a noisette, Maréchal Niel, one of the first hardy yellow roses, 'More precious and more welcome a thousand times than those Golden Roses which popes have sent to favoured kings.'

Many of the new species had a longer flowering season, and would bloom from early summer until 'the Christmas bells ring out in the winter wind'. Pot-grown roses were prized for flowering out of season.

*The Pergola, Brantwood, Surbiton.*

*Shirley Hibberd's favourite climbers included Dundee Rambler, Belle de Bordeaux and Princess Louise Victoria. Dorothy Perkins, the 'strong growing climber', was introduced in 1901 and became an instant favourite.*

# THE ROSARY

*A patent long-handled device for pruning roses (right); 'As a structural embellishment to a rose garden, nothing can be more appropriately introduced than a rose-temple, of which a very elegant form, designed by Mr W. Rendle, of Victoria Street, London, is represented in the accompanying woodcut.'*

Robert Thompson

Rose Temple, by Rendle

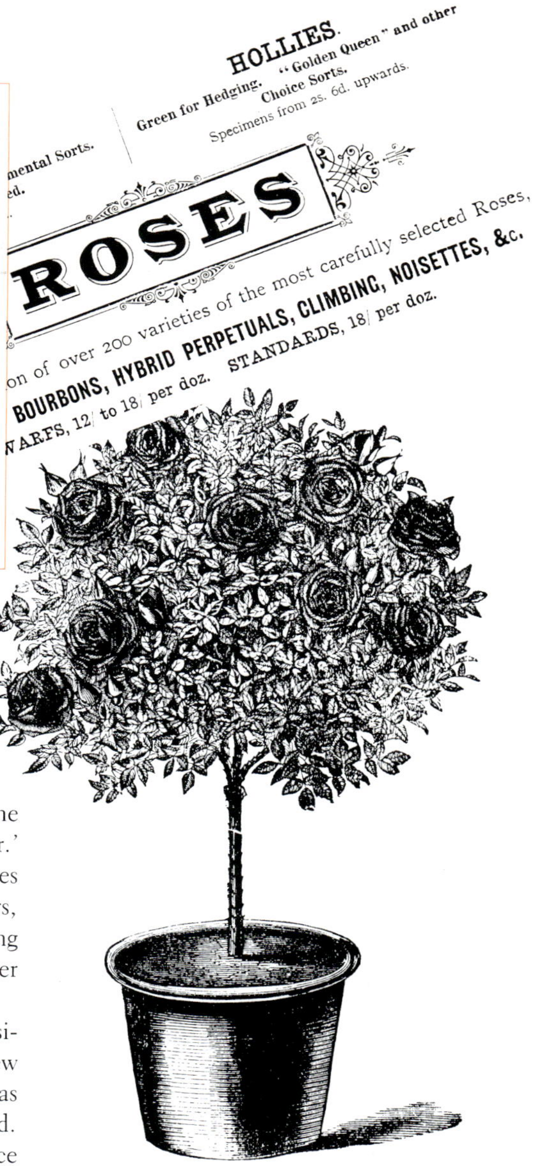


LIKE all Victorians, Shirley Hibberd preferred roses to be planted in a rosary, apart from other flowers. A rosary should be symmetrical in form, with beds no wider than five feet (in order to pick, prune, label and admire without trampling the soil), the ideal centrepiece being an arbour or pavilion. This might be raised so that the glory of the garden was viewed as a whole. The alternative merits of grass and gravel walks were debated: 'The green sward is refreshing to the eyes after these have been gazing upon the brilliant hues of the flowers: in fact the predominant colour of a rosary is red, and of this green is complementary,' stated one authority. 'The only objection to grass walks is that they are unpleasant to walk upon early in the morning, late in the evening, and after wet weather.' Where the walks intersected, arches for climbers were favoured. Pillars, standards and roses trained along swags of rope or chain were other possible features.

For the boundary Hibberd considered 'a rich dark line of clipped yew or glistening holly', invaluable as both a shelter and a background. Dean Hole wrote that at the entrance to the garden 'I would have the approaches made purposely obscure and narrow, that the visitor may come with a sudden gladness and wonder upon the glowing scene, as the traveller by rail emerges from a dark tunnel into the brightness of day and a fair landscape: or as some dejected whist-player finds, at the extremity of wretched cards, the ace, king and queen of trumps.'

## THE ROSARY

*Shirley Hibberd's design for a rosarium (left). He recommended that the roses be sheltered from the north and west by a belt of shrubbery.*

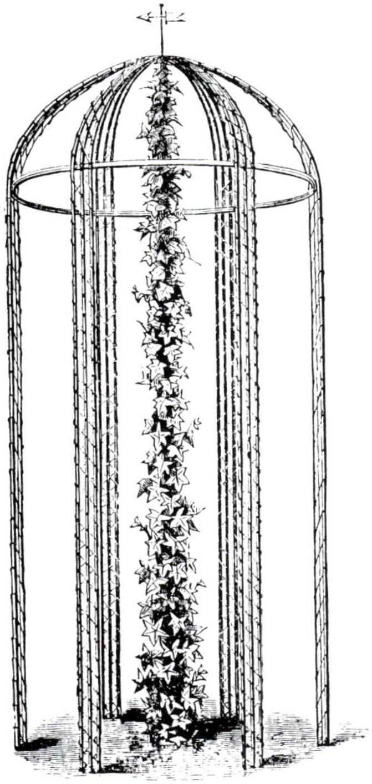

TRELLIS PAVILION FOR PILLAR ROSES.

ROSE PILLAR, FURNISHED.

*The vivid crimson General Jacqueminot and Duchess of Norfolk were both popular choices for pillar roses.*

# BEDS AND BEDDING

*The coloured plates for carpet bedding are from* The Gardener's Assistant *(1878) by Robert Thompson. He gave classified and select lists of plants with blue, carmine, crimson, glaucous, green, orange-red, purple, white and yellow leaves.*

*'Plans that may serve either for architectural or common flower gardens', from Loudon.*

THE PATIENCE and deftness of the Victorian gardener were tested to the limits when raising the many hundreds of plants that were used for bedding out. Plants too tender to survive the winter out of doors were kept under cover until they were transferred to a flower bed in early summer. The plants – pelargonium, calceolaria, petunia, verbena, salvia – came originally from South America and South Africa. They were planted out in scrupulously ordered pentagons, hexagons, parallelograms and rhomboids to create beds of unexceptionable neatness and brilliance, visible from the drawing-room windows or from the terrace.

The skills involved in bedding out extended from planning the overall geometrical layout of the beds, and transferring the design from paper on to the ground, to choosing the plants to create both harmony and contrast and to raising them. A similar proficiency was required in the archetypally Victorian form of seasonal planting known as carpet bedding. Dense patterns were made up of dwarf or creeping foliage plants, with coloured leaves – among them coleus, sedum and sempervivum. These were clipped to maintain the design, which might be of a heraldic device, or even a butterfly.

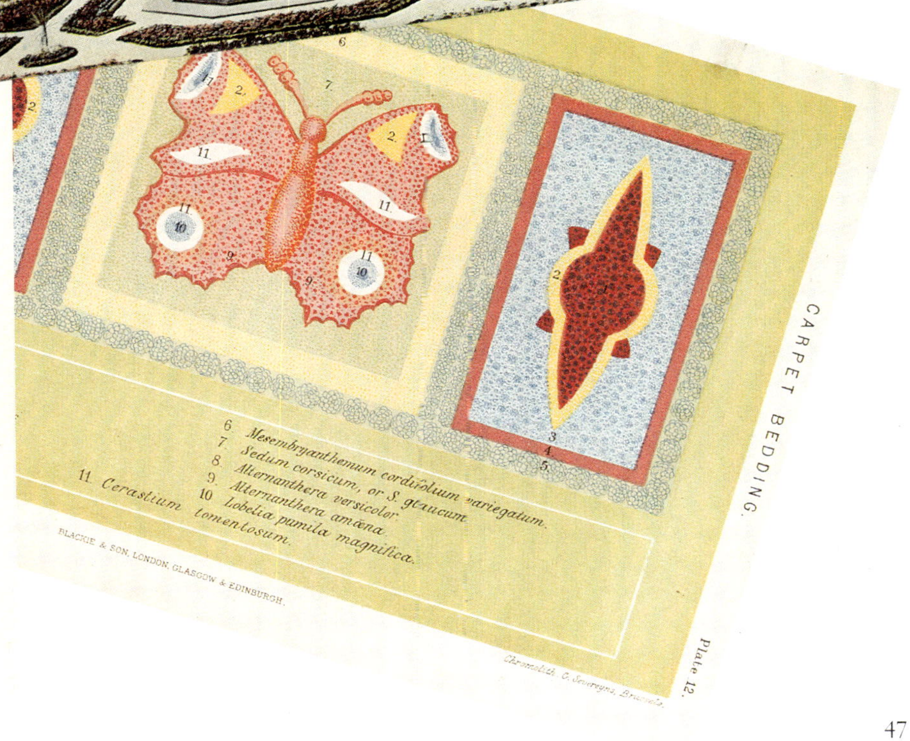


## BEDS AND BEDDING

*The designs were laid out using a giant compass.*

# Gardening for Ladies

*Book plates for two lady gardeners with vignettes of idyllic gardens.*

EVERY
LADY HER OWN
FLOWER GARDENER,
BY
LOUISA JOHNSON.
A NEW EDITION.
LONDON.
PUBLISHED BY WM S. ORR & Co PATERNOSTER ROW.
MDCCCXL.

*'I dedicate it to all of my own sex who delight in flowers.'*
Louisa Johnson

MRS LOUDON took a robust view of the capabilities of women as gardeners. 'It must be confessed,' she wrote at the beginning of *Gardening for Ladies*, 'that digging appears at first sight, a very laborious employment, and one particularly unfitted to small and delicately formed hands and feet'; but she continued, 'by a little attention to the principles of mechanics and the laws of motion, the labour may be much simplified and rendered comparatively easy'. Not only would the lady gardener

*Ladies bedding out plants.*

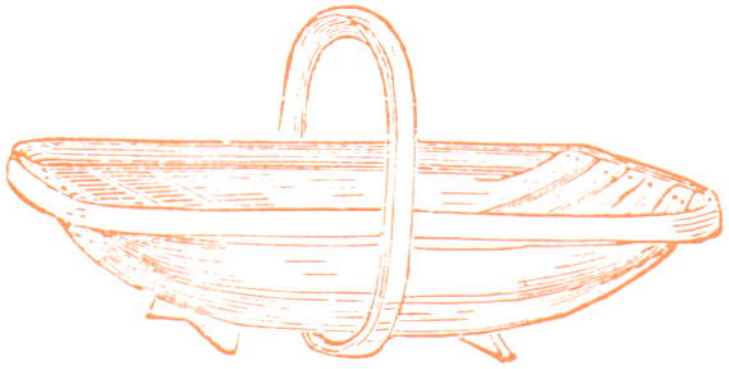

have the satisfaction of seeing the garden created by the labour of her own hands, 'but she will find her health and spirits wonderfully improved by the exercise, and by the refreshing smell of the fresh earth'. Later in the book she conceded, in line with such authors as Louisa Johnson, that whatever the practicability that might be entertained of a woman attending to the culture of culinary vegetables and fruit trees, her pre-eminent responsibility was always for the management of the flower garden.

# Bees in the Garden

Diligence and industry are the virtues of the bee, qualities that greatly appealed to the Victorians, who delighted in the 'little labourers'.

Observatory hives were situated in conservatories and greenhouses, or even simply attached to windows, through which their activities could be viewed.

'Fancy yourself to be in a pretty cottage garden on a hot summer's morning . . . you have chosen the shadiest nook under the old walnut-tree . . . then you notice a gentle buzzing close to you and see that close by, several bees are working busily among the flowers.' So was the bees' business of collecting the nectar and pollinating the flowers described in *The Fairy-land of Science*.

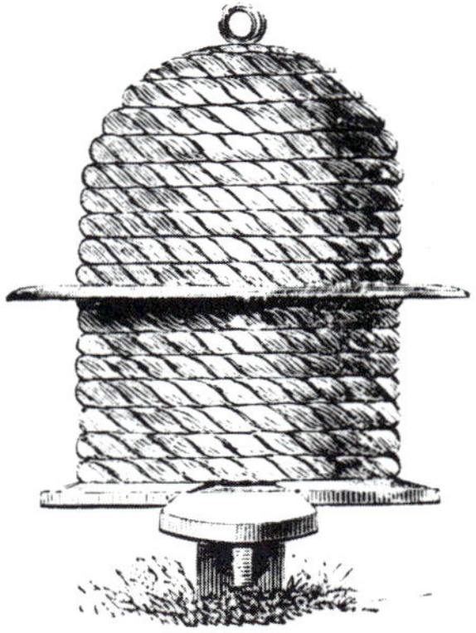

*This plaited straw beehive was perched on a pedestal to prevent depredation by vermin.*

*'In All Labour There Is Profit', read the motto beneath the engraving of a bee shed near Halstead, Essex.*

# BEES IN THE GARDEN

THE MALE, OR DRONE, BEE

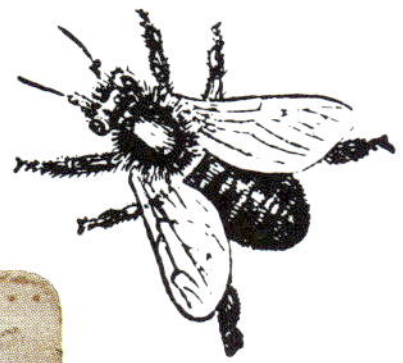

THE COMMON, OR WORKING, BEE

Besides the amusement of watching bees at their work, were the practical advantages of keeping them. Beeswax and honey were used in polishes as well as for sweetening and for medicinal purposes Ladies were urged to steal an hour day from their indoor pursuits for the management of the hives, choosing between the plaited, straw or sheaved hives that lasted a summer and the more permanent wooden ones.

The beekeeper's garden would be planted with orchard trees; gooseberry, raspberry and currant bushes; clover; wallflowers; borage; bugloss; rosemary and thyme.

THE QUEEN, OR MOTHER, BEE

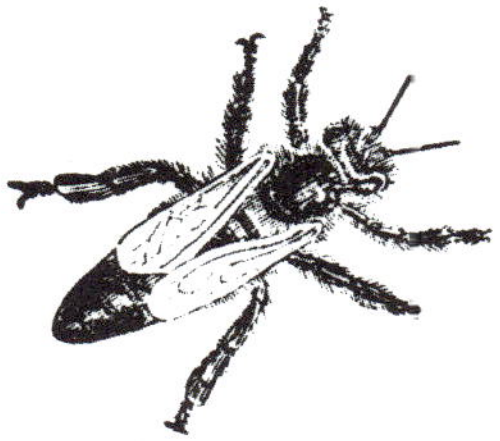

# THE KITCHEN GARDEN

*Robert Thompson, in* The Gardener's Assistant, *listed a hundred different plants for the kitchen garden, from alexanders and angelica to wood sorrell and wormwood.*

THE CULINARY or kitchen garden (the *jardin potager* of the French) was planned to supply many of the needs of the household: vegetables throughout the year, fruit, pot-herbs for garnishing and seasoning, medicinal plants such as camomile and hyssop, as well as rhubarb, horse-radish and flowers for cutting.

Readers of Robert Thompson's *The Gardener's Assistant* were assumed to belong to the new generation of 'mansion-builders'. His advice to them was that the kitchen garden

*A home-made seed packet: kale was also known as borecole.*

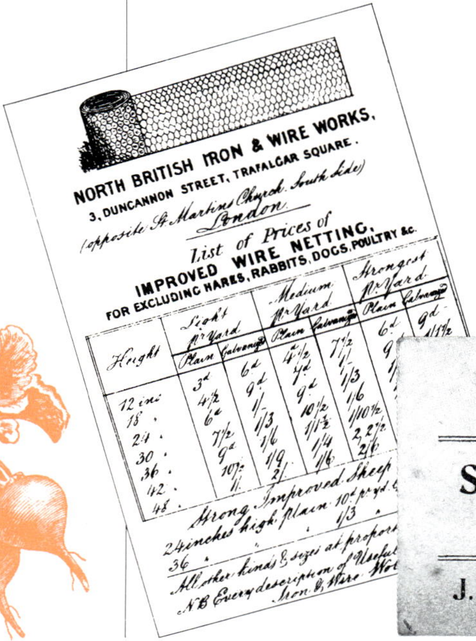


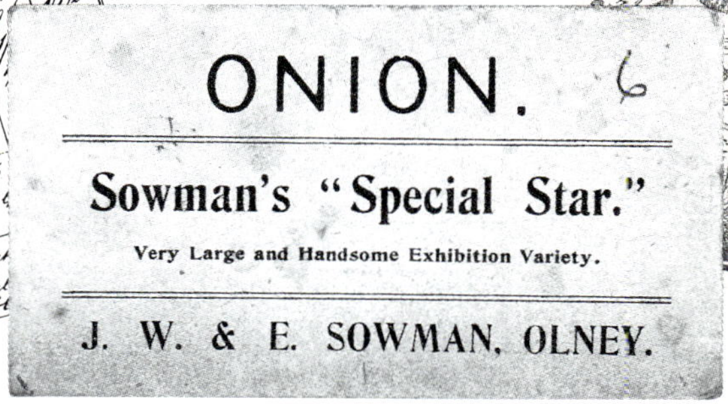


*Radishes.*

should be so near the house 'as to be conveniently accessible on foot, probably within little more than a quarter of a mile; while it should be so distant as to avoid the possibility of offence arising from the necessary gardening operations, and the resort of workmen'. It should not on any account be visible from the house or lawn and, wherever it was placed, should be masked by shrubs. The ideal kitchen garden had straight gravel paths, suitable for wheeling heavy loads or carting, bordered with box and espaliered fruit trees.

*Not less than an acre was calculated to 'afford a moderate supply for 16 persons'.*

# Growing Vegetables

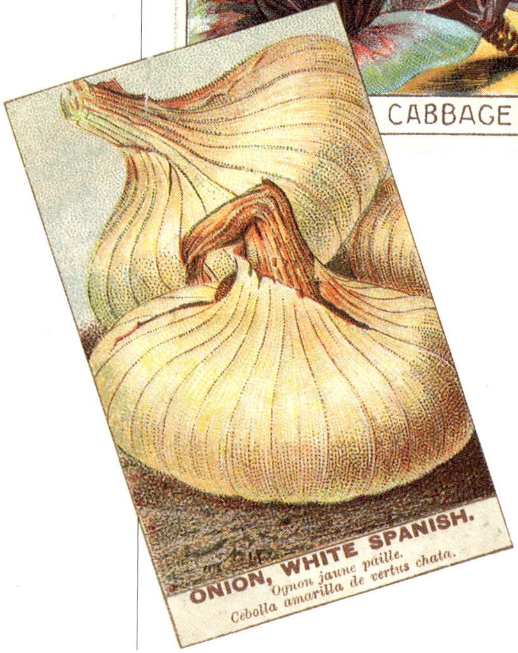

*Seed packets for onions and spring onions, red pickling cabbage and crimson globe beet.*

ORDER and science were the key to successful vegetable gardening, it was said, contrasting with the romance and sentiment that was apt to creep into the creation of flower gardens and pleasure grounds. Experience, in the opinion of the seed merchant Thomas M'Kenzie of Belfast and Dublin, counted for all. 'Simple though the cultivation of vegetables is considered by many, yet to grow them to perfection requires a skill acquired only by experience – book learning as the gardener would call it, may teach leading principles, but there are many minor requirements with which the Amateur can only become familiar by experience.'

One of the tips offered to the novice in Charles M'Intosh's *Book of the Garden* concerned the sowing of onions in conjunction with other vegetables: 'a little lettuce-seed may be thinly scattered over the ground after the onions are sown and many of them may be transplanted'. And he remarked that 'in soils where carrots are destroyed by grub, they often, when sown along with onions or leeks, escape their attacks'. The origin of many of these theories was, according to M'Intosh, 'the ancients' who 'believed that some plants had a sympathy with, or antipathy to each other'. They also regulated their sowing, planting and gathering of crops so that they fitted in with certain stages of the lunar cycle.

Onions, when about the size of a writing-quill, were devoured in astonishing quantities by the humbler classes. Other labourers' fare was the potato, cabbage, leek, turnip, and the bean, the traditional accompaniment to bacon. (Par-boiled beans in a weak syrup of honey and musk made excellent bait for fish.) By the end of the century tomatoes, or 'love apples' as they were called, were not only grown at large establishments, where French cooks reigned supreme in the kitchen, but in the gardens of amateurs and cottagers as well.

*A family working in their vegetable garden, a painting by William Small, 1871.*

# Pests and Weeds

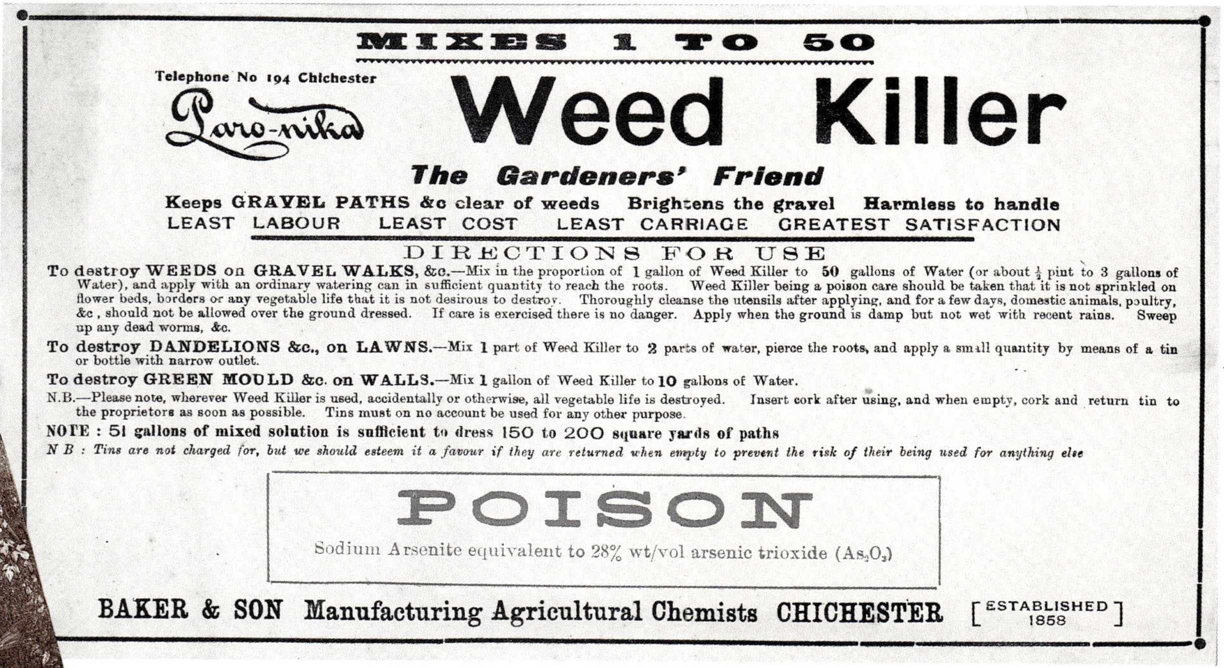

*A gentleman and lady spraying with a garden syringe.*

Grub of the cockchafer

Turnip flea beetle

No garden was without its enemies in the form of pests and weeds. 'The smaller the garden the more likely it is to be infested with snails, slugs and wood-lice,' wrote Shirley Hibberd; 'every inch of paling, wall, and even rock-work, will become a harbour for vermin unless the gardener be vigilant both in destroying and preventing.' The intolerable nuisance of slugs and snails could be combated by luring them with cabbage leaves and then consigning them to a pot of salty water; another method was to apply one of the patent preparations such as the deadly Slugene.

There were fumigators and sulphurators, for freeing plants from infestation in the greenhouse and conservatory, and a variety of pumps, syringes and sprays for dispensing the poisons; a model with a cut-glass bottle and nickel-plated top was designed specially for ladies.

Onion fly

# Pests and Weeds

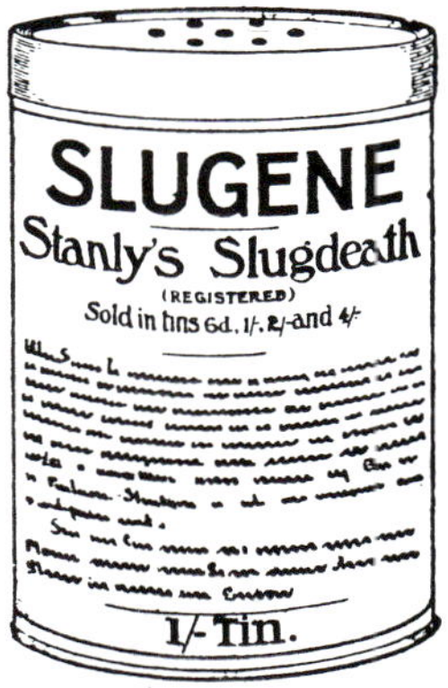


'Slugene is a complete antidote against slugs, and will not injure the tenderest vegetation. It is in powder, and a few grains are sufficient to penetrate any of the species found above ground.' Tins 6d to 4/-.

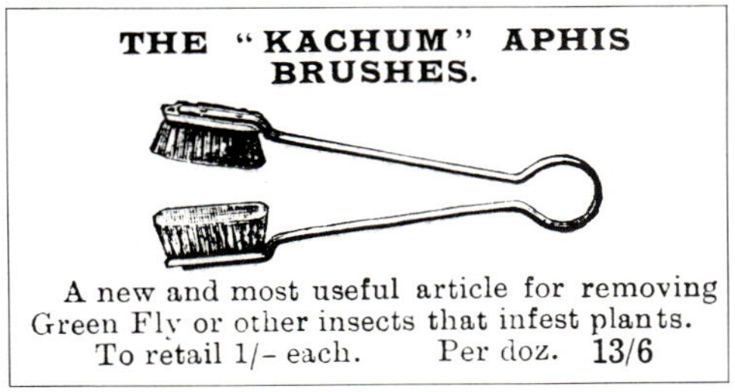


*The Aphis Brush was invented by the Rev. E. S. Bull of Colchester for removing aphids from his roses without injuring them.*

*Dandelion leaves were blanched and eaten in salads.*

# Cottage Gardens

*Mignonettes were described by W. D. Drury as being 'much prized for cutting as they emit such a delightful perfume'.*

THE ABUNDANCE and simplicity of the cottage garden was one of the glories of England: straight, economically spaced rows of vegetables, clumps of rosemary and lavender, sweet william, pinks and mignonette seeded randomly beside hollyhocks, foxgloves and still taller sunflowers. 'The cool breeze as it enters the open casement is but just strong enough to fan the fresh incense of the Cabbage Roses into the room.'

Mary Howitt saw the cottager's lot (by comparison with that of the rich man) as one of singular contentment:

*Around the rich man's trellised bower*
*Gay, costly creepers run:*
*The poor man has his scarlet-beans*
*To screen him from the sun.*

*And there before the little bench*
*O'ershadowed by the bower,*
*Grow southernwood and lemon-*
*thyme,*
*Sweet-pea and gillyflower;*

*And here on sabbath evenings,*
*Until the stars are out,*
*With a little one in either hand,*
*He walketh all about.*

*For though his garden plot is small,*
*Him doth it satisfy;*
*For there's no inch of all his ground*
*That does not fill his eye.*

*'Sweet-scented jasmine and woodbine, purple clematis and monthly roses fight lovingly for a place beside the rustic porch', as seen in a series of postcards published by Raphael Tuck & Sons.*

The resourcefulness of the cottage gardener was frequently admired. Anne Cobbett remarked upon the use of oyster shells, 'laid with the outer side upward, and in a straight line with one another, to form an edging for the path'; or else, 'the shank-bone of sheep, thrust into the earth till within an inch of the joint and packed so closely as to look like one continuous piece of carved bone'.

Beside the cottage door might hang the cage of a songbird, whose voice would sound through the garden from early morning till nightfall: a canary, a thrush or a linnet.

*A holliyhock on a Valentine.*

# Mowing the Lawn

*The Automaton 'goes easily and quickly, in and out of cut, and does its work beautifully. I consider it as near perfection as possible. I like the way the knives are set, as they are very easily got at, and can be set firm to a nicety.'*

The King's Cross

# Mowing the Lawn

The New Patent Speedwell

The Mercury 888

The Newer Easy

Edwin Budding worked in the cloth trade. One day, observing the rotating blades used in shaving the nap of cloth, he realized that the principle could be adapted to cutting grass; so, in 1830, the lawnmower was invented.

'No pleasure garden can be very handsome without a green-sward,' wrote Anne Cobbett in 1842. 'Even in a small ground of not more than an acre or so, the effect of the green-sward with borders of flowers or flowering shrubs, is preferable to a mere display of flowers however brilliant. England is famed all over the world for its beautiful turf.'

All kinds of machine were devised to achieve this excellence, patent succeeding patent. Ransome's Anglo-Paris was designed for small gardens and for ladies; Green's Patent Noiseless was in constant use in the royal gardens; the New Monarch was for tennis courts; the Multum in Parvo for narrow strips around flower beds. For larger lawns there were double-handled mowers (for man and boy) and ones drawn by horses. A model manufactured by Green's made little noise and could be used next to the most spirited animal without fear of it running away. Leather boots, sold in sets of four, prevented hoofprints on the lawn.

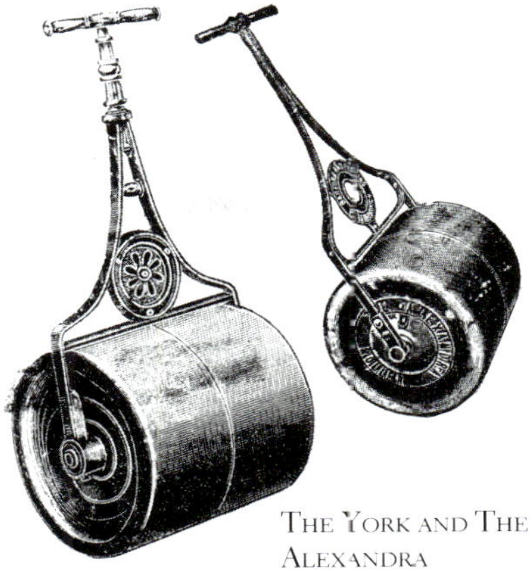

The York and The Alexandra

*Green's also offered sand and water-ballast rollers and the Improved Revolving Sprinkler.*

# GAMES ON THE LAWN

*'The Tennis Party' by Charles Gere.*

*Both tennis and croquet were just as popular with the ladies as the gentlemen.*

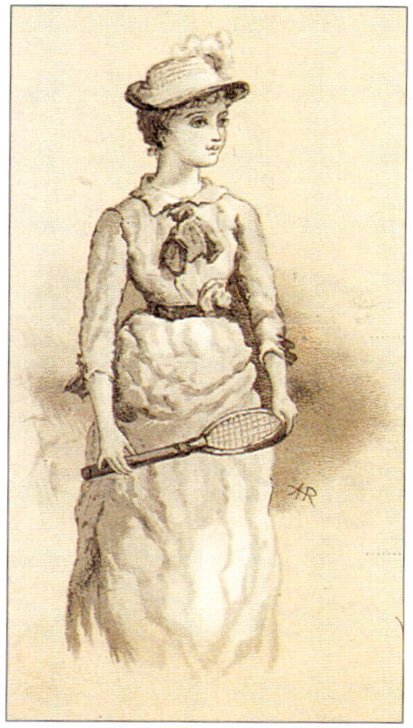

FROM the garden would rise the sound of laughter and exclamations of enjoyment and dismay as games of tennis, bowls and croquet were played on the grass.

'On the lawn of many a country house may yet be seen that remnant of barbarism, the old-fashioned net with guy-ropes, than which nothing can be more utterly objectionable or calculated to spoil both the game and one's temper,' wrote Mrs Hillyard on the subject of tennis in *The Gentlewoman's Book of Sports*. She recalled playing at a house where two fox-terriers had been trained to retrieve the balls from the bushes and flower beds. Each dog took his own end of

the court, positioned well behind the base-line, and, although the court was in the middle of a large lawn, never a ball was lost during the whole afternoon.

For bowls it was necessary to have a smooth turf entirely free from weeds and such impediments to accuracy as wormcasts. The bowling green was frequently created in a sunken panel, which, as the practical Mr Thompson observed in *The Gardener's Assistant*, could be flooded in winter and, in frosty weather, converted into a skating ground. A border of mixed evergreen and deciduous flowering shrubs in the immediate surroundings served both as a screen and as decoration.

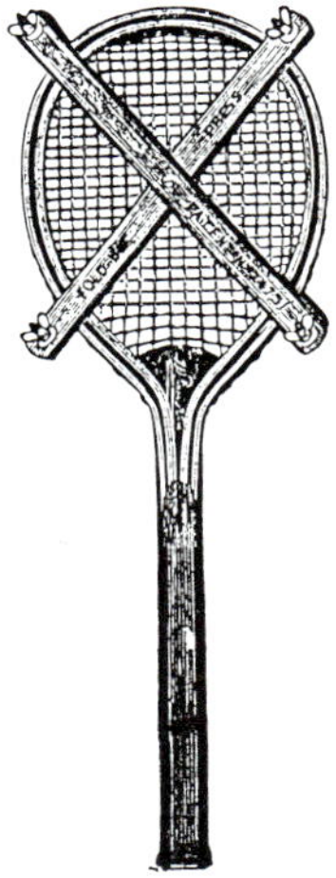

# GAMES ON THE LAWN

*The Patent Fold-up Racquet Press; invitation to a tennis party; cabinet photograph by G. Churchill, 'Photographer to Her Majesty the Queen & most of the Imperial & Royal Families of Europe'*; carte-de-visite *of a croquet party, photographed in London.*

'The universal taste for lawns' was credited in *The Popular Recreator* to the sporting and social opportunities offered by croquet. 'It has been said that there is "nothing like a good hater"; if so, society owes a vast debt to croquet for affording so many opportunities . . . of indulging in that very amiable passion'. The croquet lawn stood 'in the same relation to well-appointed gardens as billiards-rooms to luxurious houses'. Here, though, the ladies would play as equals with gentlemen.

# A CHILD'S GARDEN

*Children were admonished, 'Grow nothing carelessly; whatever is worth growing at all is worth growing well.'*

WEEDS AND FLOWERS.

DEAR children, the flowers you are busied about,
Will grow though they toil not nor [spin;
And while you are tending the garden without,
You should think of the garden with- [in.
The heart is by nature like wilderness ground,
Which yields neither flowers nor fruit;
There, poisonous weeds and rank thistles abound,
Which only God's hand can uproot.
Oh, seek that His Spirit this desolate place
May make like a garden to bloom;
There plant and there nurture the flowers of His grace,
In beauty and lasting perfume.

*A cabinet photograph of a child with a miniature wheelbarrow.*

THE PLEASURE of gardening for children was clearly recognized by the Victorians. They saw that for children whole gardens full of gorgeous flowers grown by others did not give half the joy of even a tiny corner aglow with the results of their own efforts. Anne Cobbett, who concerned herself with the upbringing of children among other matters, was of the opinion that they would be captivated by the forms and colours of blossom even before their tongues could express admiration. Gardening, an amusement so cheering and healthy, would stand them in good stead for the whole of their lives, she maintained. Jane Loudon commented on the need for children to have their gardens in an open airy position, with plenty of light. She warned against leaving it to the gardener who 'very frequently assigns them some position of ground which is unfit for any other purpose.'

Various texts on the subject of gardening for the young were published by the Society for Promoting Christian Knowledge. The Rev. C. A. Johns seemed in no doubt that gardening taught children 'to look into and admire the very humblest of God's works'. The same frost that made it necessary to pursue occupations indoors was sent by God to prepare the soil for seeds. Sermonizing further, he wrote, 'You already, I doubt not, anticipate great pleasure in gathering nosegays from plants raised from seeds sown by yourselves in your own gardens . . . From having watched them come into leaf and bud, and flower, and from having seen how entirely dependent they are on the dew of God's Providence, you will value them as gifts from Himself, bestowed in fulfilment of His promise, to reward your industry and patience.'

*A Victorian valentine.*

75

QUAILS AND YOUNG.

MR. QUAIL and Mrs. Quail, and all the little quails,

## A CHILD'S GARDEN

# Garden Furniture

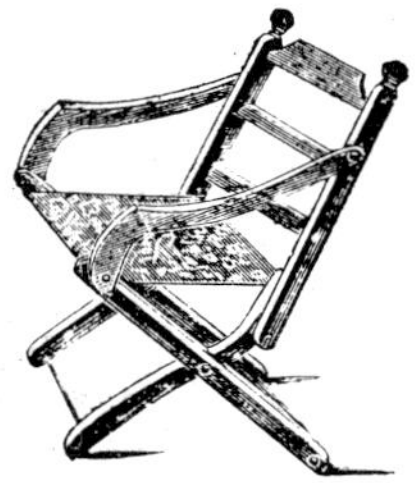

The Gent's Croquet, varnished birch with carpet seat, 3/9d

The Folding Hammock Chair, canvas seat and canopy, 5/7½d

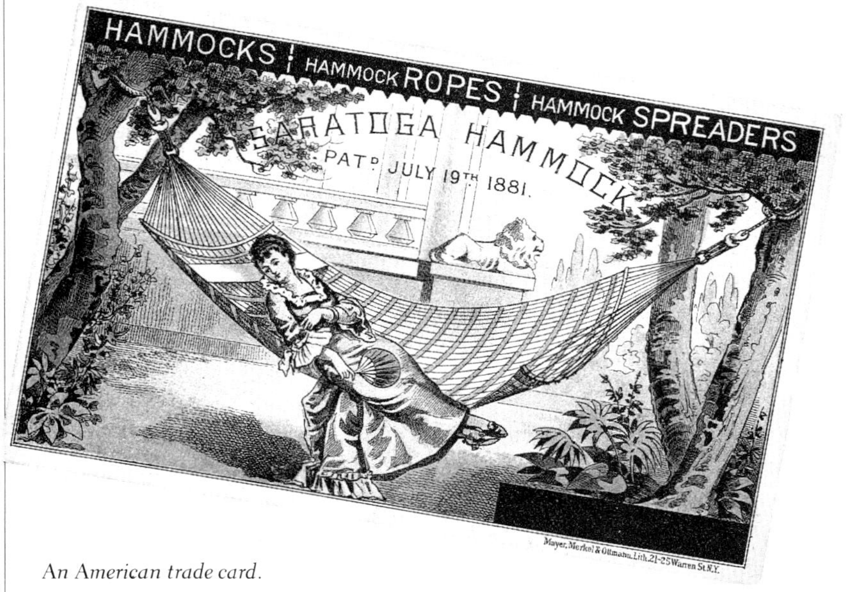


*An American trade card.*

Chairs and tables, hammocks and umbrellas, designed for open-air use, permitted the Victorian lady – constricted by tightly laced stays and perhaps a patent folding bustle – to comport herself decorously in the garden. Tea on the lawn, a quiet moment spent swinging gently beneath the leaves of trees: these were images of summertime.

Cast-iron furniture was popular and could conveniently be left out of doors. Tables, circular or rectangular and with the choice of a marble top, were offered for sale by such manufacturers as O'Brien, Thomas & Co. of London at 17/6d (2/5d extra if bronzed). Newer models had a chessboard top and a holder for sticks and umbrellas. Tennis and croquet chairs were supplied in two weights, 'strong' and 'light', the wrought-iron framework painted green.

The summer season catalogue of W. B. Fordham & Sons of King's Cross, London, specialists in 'Garden and Sporting Requisites', had a line in bamboo furniture, including teatables with folding flaps with which

**THE "ASCOT" UMBRELLA,**

Diameter, 6 ft.

| | | 5 | 6 | 8 | 10 ribs |
|---|---|---|---|---|---|
| Grey ... | each | 18/- | 19/6 | 21/6 | 25/6 |
| Striped .... | ,, | — | 22/6 | 24/6 | 26/3 |
| Best Striped | ,, | — | — | 27/- | 33/- |

Tables, extra ... ... ... each 9/-

If hinged to adjust to any angle, 9/9 extra.

**CANE FOLDING LOUNGES.**

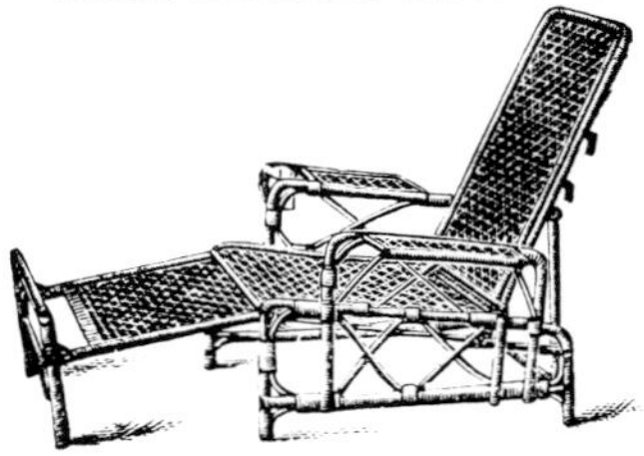

The Very Best Quality Cane.

Suitable for the Garden, for Invalids, Deck Lounges, Hospitals, Sanatoriums, &c.

| | Each |
|---|---|
| Plain Cane, with hole in arm rest for glass | 36/- |
| Plain and Malacca Cane (Mixed) with glass hole ... ... ... ... | 31/6 |

Either of the above can be supplied with Book Box at side, extra 4/6

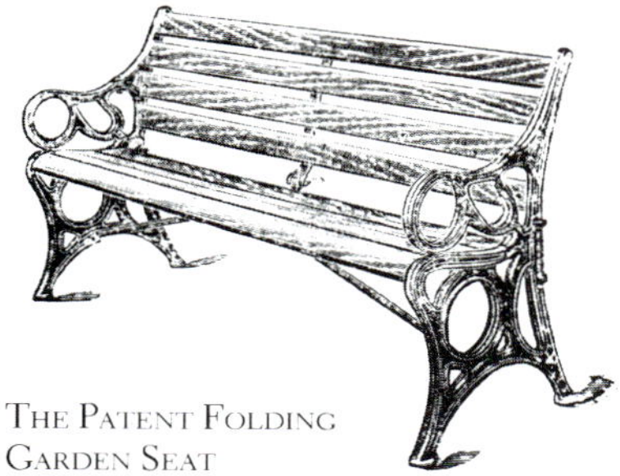

The Patent Folding Garden Seat

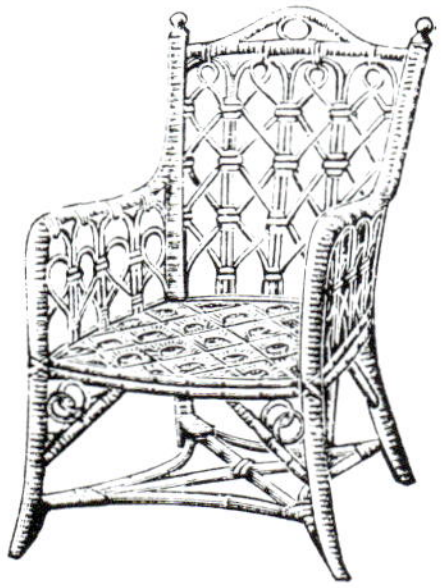

The Rattan Cane Arm Chair

the Simplex table-cloth clamp, 'a neat and very ingenious clip for preventing the table cloth being blown off', might be used. A simple hammock cost 10/- and came complete with plaid cover and fixed upholstered pillow with buttons and tassels; the Siesta Self-opening Automatic Hammock cost 26/-.

Wooden furniture in a rustic style was popular, but it was roughly made of timber that retained the bark. Shirley Hibberd admonished his readers that it gave the appearance of a tea garden in a suburban tavern.

*More exotic garden furniture included a wirework love seat (above) and a double hammock (right).*

The Canted Matting Table

## Garden Furniture

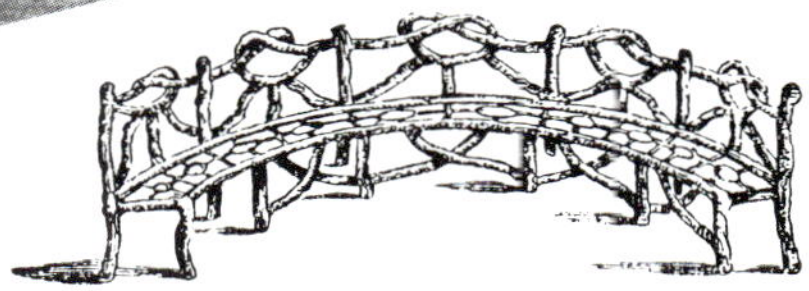

*A rustic seat illustrated in* Rustic Adornments for Homes of Taste *by Shirley Hibberd.*

## HERBACEOUS BORDERS

*This American nurseryman offered perennial ornamental grasses as well as valerian and thrift.*

# Herbaceous Borders

Quintessentially Victorian were the mixed borders that came into fashion in the later years of the Queen's reign. They were described by Shirley Hibberd in *The Amateur's Flower Garden* as 'a comfortable home for beautiful flowers'. The borders imitated the profusion and variety found in cottage gardens, and they were first made popular by William Robinson, author of *The English Flower Garden*, and then later by Gertrude Jekyll.

The plants that gave the borders their character – and their name – were the herbaceous perennials: lilies, irises, hollyhocks, delphiniums, phlox, peonies and potentillas. The glory of herbaceous borders lay in the juxtaposition and blending of colour, height and mass, and the luxuriance of the flowers and their foliage. Gertrude Jekyll favoured hot colours at the centre, shading into cooler ones at each end.

The labour of watering, mulching and staking the plants was generously repaid during the month or two for which the display was in full bloom. In the words of Robinson, 'a simple border has been the first expression of flower gardening and there is no arrangement of flowers more graceful, varied or capable of giving more delight'.

*'A London Garden in August', from* Gardens of England.

*'Old English Garden Flowers', cigarette cards of hardy perennials issued by W. D. & H. O. Wills early this century. On the reverse is invaluable information on the cultivation of plants.*

# GARDEN BUILDINGS

*'Seat shades, summerhouses, and what our continental neighbours term "kiosks" can be made to form not only useful ornaments, but exceedingly attractive features', wrote Samuel Wood, illustrating the incomplete seat shade (below).*

SUMMERHOUSES: the mere mention of them 'brings to mind a vision of damp boards, earwigs, spiders and mildew', wrote W. S. Rogers. 'How then can the summerhouse be made a comfortable, useful and ornamental retreat amidst our flowers? First it must be weather-proof', he declared. 'Then it must be unpretentious in design and free from trumpery embellishments. The use of stained and varnished tree branches, interlaced to form a "rustic" pattern,

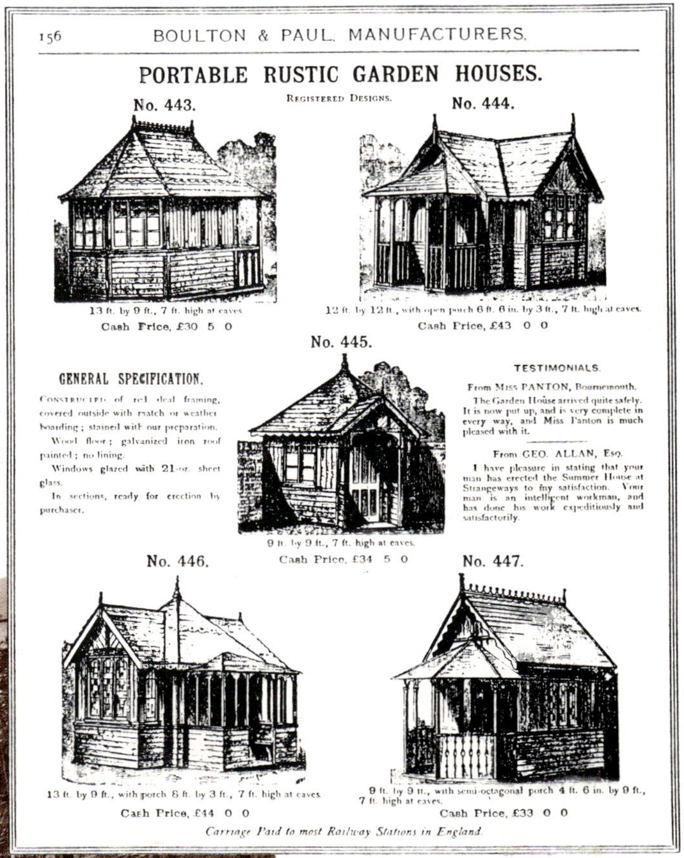

156 BOULTON & PAUL. MANUFACTURERS.

PORTABLE RUSTIC GARDEN HOUSES.

REGISTERED DESIGNS.

No. 443.

13 ft. by 9 ft., 7 ft. high at eaves.

Cash Price, £30 5 0

No. 444.

12 ft. by 12 ft., with open porch 6 ft. 6 in. by 3 ft., 7 ft. high at eaves.

Cash Price, £43 0 0

No. 445.

9 ft. by 9 ft., 7 ft. high at eaves.

Cash Price, £34 5 0

GENERAL SPECIFICATION.

CONSTRUCTED of red deal framing, covered outside with match or weather boarding; stained with our preparation.

Wood floor; galvanized iron roof painted; no lining.

Windows glazed with 21-oz. sheet glass.

In sections, ready for erection by purchaser.

TESTIMONIALS.

From MISS PANTON, Bournemouth.

The Garden House arrived quite safely. It is now put up, and is very complete in every way, and Miss Panton is much pleased with it.

From GEO. ALLAN, Esq.

I have pleasure in stating that your man has erected the Summer House at Strangeways to my satisfaction. Your man is an intelligent workman, and has done his work expeditiously and satisfactorily.

No. 446.

13 ft. by 9 ft., with porch 6 ft. by 3 ft., 7 ft. high at eaves.

Cash Price, £44 0 0

No. 447.

9 ft. by 9 ft., with semi-octagonal porch 4 ft. 6 in. by 9 ft., 7 ft. high at eaves.

Cash Price, £33 0 0

*Carriage Paid to most Railway Stations in England.*

*A Victorian family proudly photographed with their aviary.*

is a practice that had best be allowed to die out.' Rogers wrote *Villa Gardens* at the very end of Queen Victoria's reign, throughout which the rustic embellishments that he abhorred had been regarded as entirely fitting for garden buildings.

The moss houses described by Mrs Loudon in *Gardening for Ladies* were extreme examples of rustic work, of 'trumpery embellishment'. The frame was made from larch or spruce with the bark intact, interwoven with rods of hazel. The moss was wedged in between the rods, affording 'great scope to the exercise of fancy; not only in the design but for the arrangement of moss in different patterns'. (Arabesques that would resemble Turkish carpets, she suggested optimistically.) Mr Loudon was quite at odds with his wife in the matter of moss houses, dismissing them as 'generally damp, unwholesome places, fit only to be glanced at in passing... labour employed in this manner will be considered as in a great measure thrown away.'

Aviaries were fanciful buildings of another kind. Shirley Hibberd in *Rustic Adornments for Homes of Taste* illustrated a building that could be used as a birdhouse and a conservatory. 'The dome could be used as a vinery or for climbers, adding greatly to its beauty.'

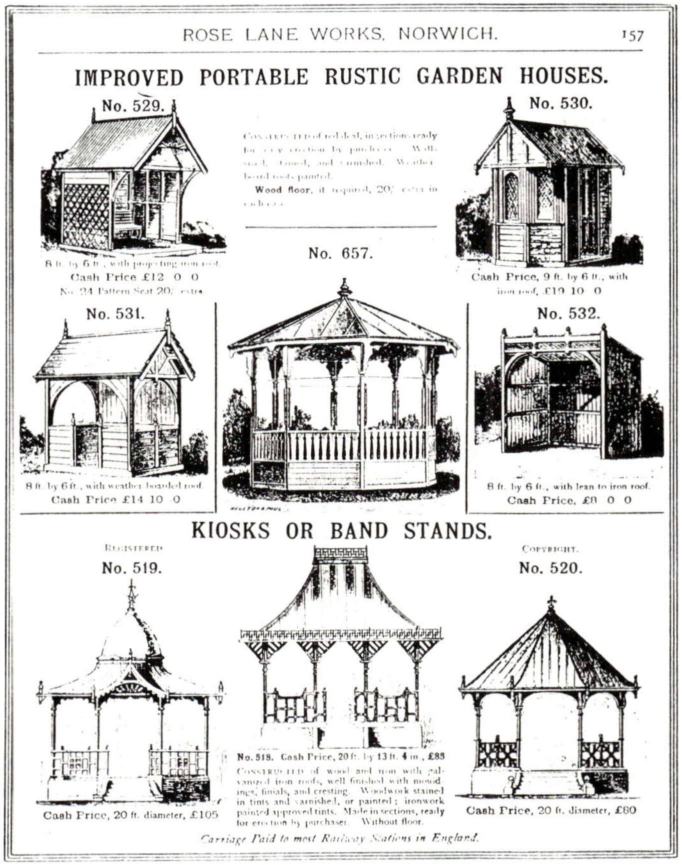

ROSE LANE WORKS, NORWICH. 157

**IMPROVED PORTABLE RUSTIC GARDEN HOUSES.**

**No. 529.**

8 ft. by 6 ft., with projecting iron roof.
Cash Price £12 0 0
No. 24 Pattern Seat 20/ extra.

**Wood floor**, if required, 20/ extra in each case.

**No. 530.**

Cash Price, 9 ft. by 6 ft., with iron roof, £19 10 0

**No. 657.**

**No. 531.**

8 ft. by 6 ft., with weather boarded roof.
Cash Price £14 10 0

**No. 532.**

8 ft. by 6 ft., with lean to iron roof.
Cash Price, £8 0 0

**KIOSKS OR BAND STANDS.**

REGISTERED
**No. 519.**

Cash Price, 20 ft. diameter, £105

**No. 518.** Cash Price, 20 ft. by 13 ft. 4 in., £88

CONSTRUCTED of wood and iron with galvanized iron roofs, well finished with mouldings, finials, and cresting. Woodwork stained in tints and varnished, or painted; ironwork painted approved tints. Made in sections, ready for erection by purchaser. Without floor.

COPYRIGHT.
**No. 520.**

Cash Price, 20 ft. diameter, £80

*Carriage Paid to most Railway Stations in England.*

## Garden Buildings

*These rustic covered seats and arbours were constructed from a variety of different woods including oak, birch and alder.*

# Summer Fruits

The gooseberry, the summer fruit that ripened first, enjoyed national popularity, and there was a generally held belief that British gooseberries had no equal anywhere in the world. The best of all were said to be grown in Scotland, where scarcely a garden was devoid of gooseberry bushes. R. Thompson, in *The Gardener's Assistant*, listed seventy-seven varieties, divided into red, yellow and green, with hispid, downy or smooth surfaces, and names such as Taylor's Bright Venus and Leigh's Rifleman. Gooseberry growers' shows attracted much local attention. The fruits, arranged in boxes, were judged on their size and weight; the traditional prize a copper kettle.

Cottages were seldom without a cherry tree in the garden, for its blossom in spring and fruit in summer: May Duke on the south or west wall of an enclosed garden and Morello, excellent for preserves and tarts, on the north.

Mrs Beeton, whose *Book of Household Management* appeared in many editions during the course of the century, gave recipes for a variety of delectable fruit pies and tarts, jellies and sorbets. Her menus included tall stemmed dishes of fresh fruit: pyramids of alternating red and white currants, cherries, raspberries, or strawberries would be piled high and placed on the table as the finale to dinner.

Some of the soft fruit was grown for making conserves which, according to Charles Dudley Warner, were 'patronized by all classes of society and ages, being especially welcomed on the tea-table by the little folks.'

*The cherry, the earliest fruiting tree: 'the cool refreshing nature of its juice renders it a universal favourite.'*

*Strawberries were recommended as a border so that a little idle picking might be done.*

Strawberry conserve was a particular favourite.

Among the popular varieties of strawberry were Keen's Seedling, the first of the large-fruited strawberries (developed in the 1820s by a market gardener in Isleworth named Michael Keen), Laxton's Noble and Sir Joseph Paxton, which were large and handsome, conical in shape, with a fine colour. Where possible they were planted on an east-west ridge so that a sequence of ripening would occur, the south-facing fruits being the first to reach the table.

*A feast of summer fruits: gooseberries, strawberries and plums.*

# TOPIARY

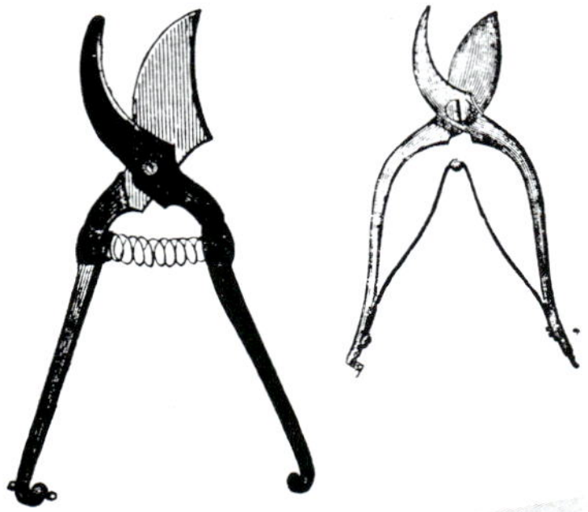

*The* sécateur lecomte *and the common* sécateur *as illustrated in* The Horticulturalist.

PEACOCKS and umbrellas, dragons and barristers' wigs: these were some of the fanciful 'living ornaments' inherited by the Victorians in gardens created by their forebears. More usual designs were balls, pyramids and cones, and the spiral and tiered columns surmounted by sitting hens, which were found in farmhouse and cottage gardens in out-of-the-way English villages.

'Verdant' or 'vegetable' sculpture, it was called; yew, box and holly the topiarist's materials. The 'absurd fashion for cutting and torturing trees into all sorts of fantastic shapes has, happily, almost passed away', it was said in the middle of the nineteenth century, but by 1891 J. D. Sedding was commending the 'quaint charm in the results of topiary art, in the prim imagery of evergreens, that all ages have felt' in his *Garden Craft Old and New*. Hedged enclosures began to return to fashion and, for elaborate figures, the branches from several plants were united by approach-grafting until a compact network of interlacing branches was growing together. The ingeniously trimmed creations introduced an element of formality, eccentricity, even humour, into the garden.

*Postcards of topiary at the turn of the century.*

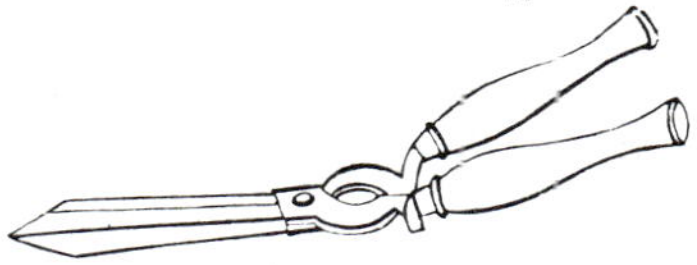

# TOPIARY

*In* The Horticulturist, *Loudon described the methods used in topiary: 'When evergreen shrubs are to be shown in common shapes, such as cones, pyramids, piers, pilasters etc., little or no training is required: but when they are to be grown into more artificial shapes, such as men or animals, the figure required is constructed of wire or trellis-work, and being placed over the plant, the shoots are confined within it; and if the plants are healthy and in good soil and situation, the figure is speedily formed.' He noted that in selecting plants for being trained into figures of men or women, it was usual to use variegated varieties for female forms.*

# Table Decorations

The fashion for floral table ornament increased in well-to-do households with the new vogue for dining *à la Russe*. The diners were waited on for the hot main courses instead of serving themselves from dishes placed in front of them on the table. 'At dinners *à la Russe*,' wrote Mrs Beeton, 'flowers occupy with the dessert the whole space unoccupied by the plates of the *convives*.'

A small tree laden with fruit appropriate to the season might grace the centre of the table, Mrs Beeton suggested, replacing the vase of flowers of daily use. 'These trees are very pretty and fashionable, and should be placed in elegant pots, of which the Pompeian patterns and colours should be selected, as relieving the monotonous brilliancy of the white table-cloth.' The asparagus fern was a particular favourite, admired for its delicate green freshness and beauty.

# TABLE DECORATIONS

For a time there was a fashion for creating a false top to the table, with holes into which pots were inserted; thus the plant appeared to grow from the table itself.

In addition to a centrepiece, small vases of flowers might be placed before each of the guests. Strongly scented flowers such as hyacinths and gardenias were generally avoided in all table decorations as they might detract from the pleasure afforded to the senses by the food.

*Trays for invalids and the tea table from Mrs Beeton.*

# Garden Ornaments

*Vases in the classical style for the terrace or Italian garden. Many were imitations of famous works of art.*

*The rustic effect was created by the use of 'old, or otherwise useless cable rope nailed on', in the case of the tub made by Mr Clowes of Manchester. It was to occupy a 'coign of vantage' in the pleasure garden rather than the terrace.*

Ornamental features in the Victorian garden ranged from urns of Classical form to tubs of a characteristically English and rustic nature, decorated with plaited osiers, bark or strips of larch.

Mrs Loudon, in *The Country Lady's Companion*, wrote of the terrace as being the bridge between the

house and the flower garden, just as the shrubbery was the link between the flower garden and the park: the terrace 'affords an admirable medium for uniting the architectural stiffness of the mansion with the beautiful wildness and grace of nature'. Steps might lead down to an 'architectural' garden, with fountains, urns and statuary; wellheads, too, were popular as centrepieces.

Ransome's Imperishable Siliceous Stone, which resisted the damage from frost, smoke and other destructive influences, was one of the artificial compounds that brought garden ornaments to a wider market: it had 'the beauty of costly sculpture at the price of ordinary cements'.

## GARDEN ORNAMENTS

*Sundials, with appropriate mottoes, were a popular feature of the late Victorian garden.*

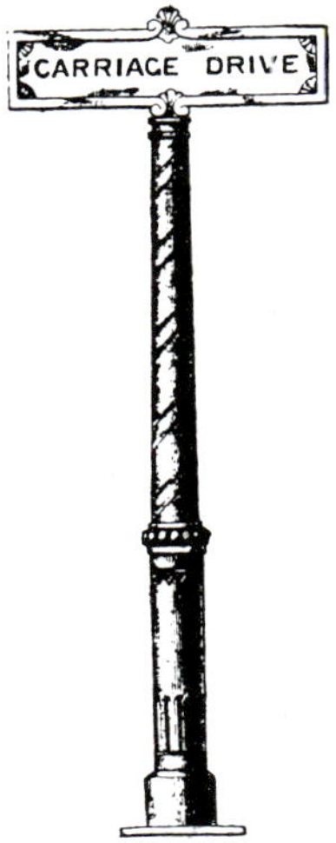

*Ornamental garden bordering.*

# Window Gardening

Much Victorian ingenuity was expended on the creation of window gardens: lattice-work balconies and window surrounds for climbers, window boxes with blinds for protection from the summer sun, miniature greenhouses inside or outside the window. Readers of Andrew Meikle's *Window Gardening in Town and Country* might have the 'quiet enjoyment of a pipe and a glass of home-brewed by their own window side.' Before their eyes was a succession of spring-flowering bulbs, mignonette, calceolaria, scarlet geranium, fuchsia and lily, leading in winter to 'a covering of British mosses, gathered from off old walls'.

Miniature greenhouses were particular favourites, hiding a bad outlook, increasing the apparent size of a room or fashionably darkening it 'with the sweet gloom of the forest.' They were purchased from a horticultural decorator at four guineas or made for an outlay of 7/6d following the instructions given in *The Popular Recreator*.

The latter also provided helpful tips for protecting plants in the greenhouse. A recommended method of combating greenfly, for instance, was to fill a cabbage stalk with shag tobacco and, to exhale the smoke, attach it to a pair of bellows.

*The Perfect, sold by Dick Radclyffe & Co, Seedsman and Horticultural Decorator, of High Holborn, London.*

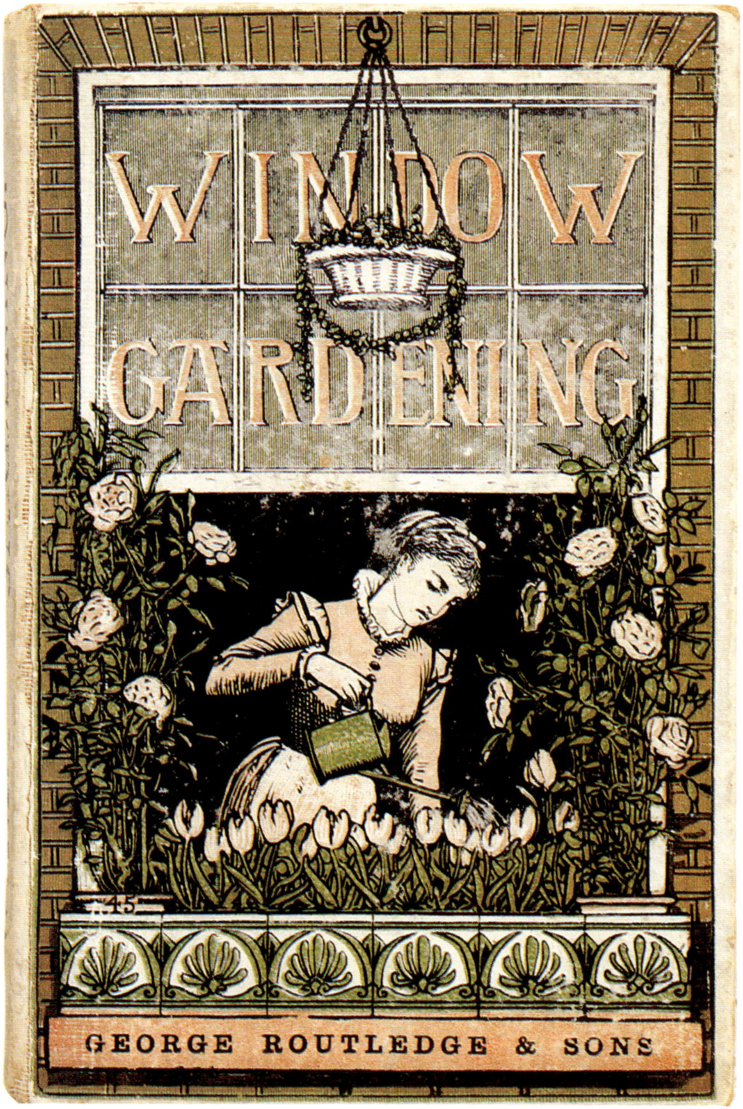


Window Gardening, *by Andrew Meikle, was 'written chiefly for the industrial classes' and so 'the plainness of the language requires no apology from me'.*

*The exterior and interior of the window garden, as illustrated in* The New Practical Window Gardener, *1877, by John R. Mollison.*

*The 'Slant Rocf' style.*

# The Water Garden

*Illustration from Robinson's* Alpine Flowers *(below): 'Water is often introduced in connection with rockwork, and high cascades may frequently be attempted, and as the supply often flows from a woody knoll it is well to take advantage of this position for the arrangement of yuccas, large grasses and herbaceous plants of noble port.'*

*Aquatic plants from C.* M'Intosh's Flower Garden. *'Flags and bullrushes disposed in groups or tufts, towards the extremity of a pool, prevent any guess or suspicion where water is to end, and do not destroy the idea of continuation.'*

## The Water Garden

Water, in the opinion of Shirley Hibberd, was the life and soul of a garden; 'it reflects the blue sky and the fleecy clouds' and 'gives a brighter verdure to the adjoining lawn, a sweeter fragrance to the neighbouring flower-border'. However, Charles M'Intosh warned his readers that any yellowness or muddiness in the water would 'excite the idea of a puddle, after a thunder-shower'.

In *Rustic Adornments for Homes of Taste*, Hibberd described the choice that was to be made, even in a small garden, between the formal arrangement, with a stone basin, fountain and circular pond shaded with rose arches and stocked with ornamental fish, and the picturesque arrangement, 'the mimic lake or river', broken in outline and with sloping banks, attended, perhaps, by water-fowl. With a pool hollowed out from the ground, he suggested that the sides should be in the form of terraces, upon which aquatic plants in pots could be placed at will. His particular favourite was 'the large white water-lily', to which 'in all water-scenery a prominent place should be given'.

*M'Intosh wrote of water lilies that 'they contribute very much to the effect of water, from the peculiarity of their forms and the richness of their masses, and may be made great use of.'*

*A combined fountain and flower bed.*

# Flower Shows

The flower show was, for many, the high point in the gardening year. Competition was fierce, whether among those who belonged to the Royal Horticultural Society (granted its royal charter by Queen Victoria in 1861) or among gardeners who were simply members of a cottage garden society. The Longford Castle Cottage Garden Society, 'like all societies of

*Prize certificates and admission tickets to horticultural shows.*

## FLOWER SHOWS

the kind,' according to Lord Radnor's head gardener, 'has for its object the promoting of a better knowledge among the people employed on the estate of the cultivation of vegetables, fruits, and flowers in their respective gardens and allotments.' Such shows were regarded with approval by the local church, which saw them as morally improving, a means of rewarding healthy outdoor endeavour. Together with prizes for the best leeks, cauliflowers and turnips were prizes for birds and rabbits, pot plants and even flower arrangements, including nosegays and buttonholes.

Among the specialist societies were the Ipswich Cucumber Society, the Dittons and District Chrysanthemum Society and the Radcliffe-on-Trent Potato Society.

*Notification of the Royal Horticultural Society Great Summer Show. The card, in the shape of a marquee, opens up to display the show in all its glory.*

# PLEASURE GROUNDS

AMOS HARPIN,

(28 YEARS GARDENER TO THE LATE F. FOX, ESQ., ELMSLEE, TOTTENHAM,)

GARDENER AND FLORIST,

KINGS' ROAD NURSERY,

TOTTENHAM.

GARDENS LAID OUT AND KEPT IN ORDER BY THE DAY, MONTH, OR YEAR.

*Every description of Trees, Plants, &c., supplied.*

*The flower of the Azalea Ledifolia.*

THE WILDERNESS, *plaisance* or pleasure ground was a separate department of the garden, at its outer limit and away from the flower beds and borders. Here grew trees and shrubs: azaleas and rhododendrons. It was a place in which to saunter and to meditate upon plants in their less constrained aspects.

In laying out the pleasure ground, Shirley Hibberd instructed his readers to 'converge the walks so that every slope forms a separate scene complete in itself, when so contemplated, and yet forming but a part of the whole'. At every opening point in the winding walk through the shrubberies, 'you will place some object to arrest the eye – a statue, a pile of rock, a fine acacia, a trained pyrus or weeping ash'. Looking well in the distance would be the tall outlines of some majestic trees.

*Cedar of Lebanon and other trees for dry situations (below).*

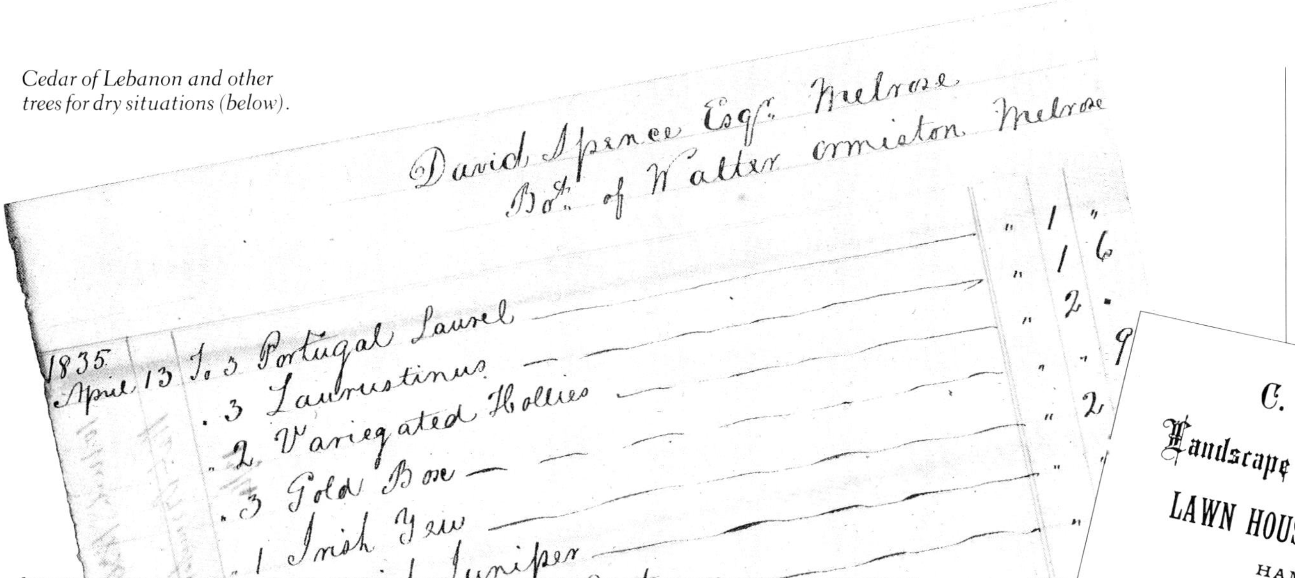
David Spence Esqr. Melrose
Bot. of Walter Ormiston Melrose

1835
April 13 To 3 Portugal Laurel
. 3 Laurustinus
. 2 Variegated Hollies
. 3 Gold Box
. 1 Irish Yew
. 1 ... Juniper

£ " 13 4

Walter Ormiston

# PLEASURE GROUNDS

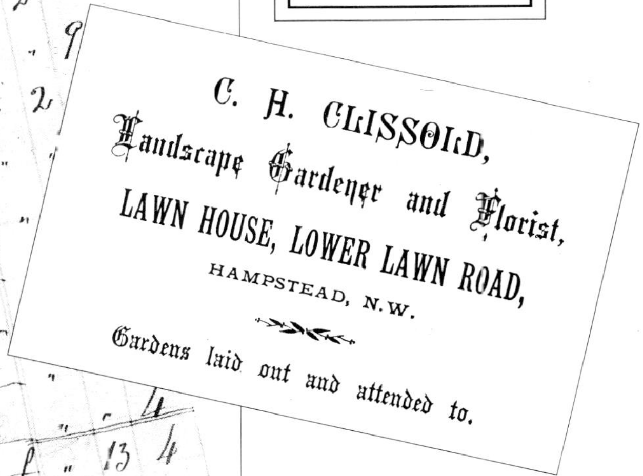
C. H. CLISSOLD,
Landscape Gardener and Florist,
LAWN HOUSE, LOWER LAWN ROAD,
HAMPSTEAD, N.W.
Gardens laid out and attended to.

*Trade cards of landscape gardeners.*

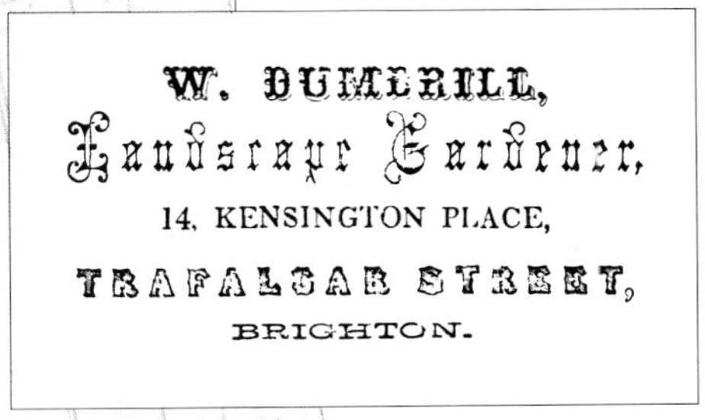
W. DUMERILL,
Landscape Gardener,
14, KENSINGTON PLACE,
TRAFALGAR STREET,
BRIGHTON.

## SEPTEMBER

VEGETABLES. – Sow the last crop of winter spinage and winter lettuces without delay; also radishes and small salads. Continue to plant for succession, cauliflower, cabbage, borecole, savoy, etc., and earth up former plantations as they advance. Take up and dry onions; clean and store them; dig up and store early potatoes. Clear the ground of all matured crops, removing all weeds and decayed matter; trench, dig, and manure the ground thus become vacant, exposing a rough surface on such as is not required for immediate cropping; hoe and stir the ground between growing crops.

FLOWERS. – If not finished last month, put in an abundant supply of cuttings of the most approved sorts of bedding plants without delay. Plant hyacinths, tulips, and crocuses in beds or borders for early flowering, and plant a few of the very early sorts in pots for forcing. Take up lilies as the foliage decays, and dry them gradually. See that gladioli and other tall growing plants are properly staked. Stake and tie the young shoots of budded roses, to secure them from strong winds; put in cuttings of China or monthly roses; transplant, prune, and train evergreens and climbers. If a new lawn is required, early in the month will be a good time to sow the grass seeds; turf may be laid for the same purpose.

FRUITS. – Gather the fruit of apples, pears, plums, etc., as they ripen, and place in a dry, airy room, which has been previously thoroughly washed and cleaned. Look over the fruit frequently, and pick out any that shows signs of decay. Rooted runners of strawberries may still be planted in lines or beds.

## OCTOBER

VEGETABLES. – In dry weather take up the main crop of potatoes; previous to storing, go over them carefully, and pick out any that may be affected with disease. Beet-root, parsnips, carrots, etc., may also be taken up and stored. Plant a good breadth of cabbages for spring use, also lettuces in warm borders. Thin out late crops of turnips, spinage, etc., and stir the soil between the rows; collect all leaves as they fall, and put in a heap sheltered from winds, or in a pit.

FLOWERS. – Clear away all annuals, biennials, and bedding plants, as they become unsightly. Before frost sets in, lift and pot any approved varieties of geraniums or other bedding plants that may be required for winter or spring stock. Where a green-house or frame is not available, they may be stored away in a light, airy room, merely giving sufficient water *to the roots* to keep them alive. Make the principal plantations of hyacinths, tulips, crocuses, snowdrops, and other spring-flowering bulbs, as the flower-beds become vacant. Transplant evergreens and shrubs.

FRUITS. – Collect and store the principal crops of apples, pears, etc.; look over those already stored, and remove any that are damaged. The transplanting of trees and bushes may be proceeded with; cuttings of gooseberries and currants may also be put in.

## NOVEMBER

VEGETABLES. – Clear the ground of cabbage stumps, pea haulms, and other matter left by exhausted crops. Trench, dig, and manure ground become vacant; leave the soil in a rough state, or in ridges exposed to the full action of the elements. Sow Dickson's First and Best peas and Mazagan beans, on well-manured ground, in a warm, sheltered border. If not completed, continue to store in dry weather, potatoes, beet-root, carrots, parsnips, and turnips. Make any alternations in the garden that may be deemed necessary. Collect all leaves to furnish a supply of leaf-mould.

FLOWERS. – Clear all flower-beds as they become unsightly; dig and manure the ground, and make any necessary alterations for the formation of the garden. Look over geraniums and other plants that have been stored away for stock; remove any decayed leaves; and give plenty of air in dry weather. Finish planting hyacinths, tulips, and other hardy bulbs for spring flowering. Plant gladioli on a porous, rich soil. Protect roses not thoroughly hardy with mats, litter, spruce branches, or other suitable covering. Prune and transplant evergreens and shrubs of all kinds. Lay down turf for lawns, croquet greens, etc.; clip and trim hedges without delay.

FRUITS. – In dry weather collect and store all fruits remaining out; examine the fruit already stored; give air to the room in mild, dry weather, taking care to exclude frost. Prune gooseberries, currants, and raspberries, and fork in a dressing of well-rotted manure round the bushes. Prune apples, pears, plums, and cherries; nail in and train any of those on the walls.

AUTUMN

# AUTUMN

RED FILBERT

On a day in mid-September Francis Kilvert made his way from Clyro, where he was curate, to nearby Bronydd. 'People at work in the orchard gathering up the windfall apples for early cider', he wrote in his diary. 'The smell of the apples very strong. Beyond the orchards the lone aspen was rustling loud and mournfully a lament for the departure of summer. Called on the old soldier. He was with his wife in the garden digging and gathering red potatoes . . . The great round red potatoes lay thick, fresh and clean on the dark newly turned mould . . . Mary Morgan brought me some apples, Sam's Crabs and Quinin's. The spring trickled and tinkled behind us and a boy from the keeper's cottage came to draw water in a blue and white jug.' This scene of early autumn was commonplace throughout the land.

Potatoes were lifted and placed with a covering of straw in a winter store or, with a covering of soil and a vent-hole stopped with straw for the release of moisture, in a mound in a well-drained part of the garden. Apples were picked and windfalls collected from beneath the trees.

AUTUMN FLOWERS

*With ruddy fruit the orchard now is*
*hung;*
*The golden hop droops pendent in the*
*breeze;*
*For Autumn from her ample hand*
*hath thrown*
*Her richest treasure on the laden trees.*

So quoted Samuel Beeton in his garden calendar for the month of September.

'Of all our fruits, the Apple is perhaps the most useful, and is appreciated by birds and beasts as well as by man', wrote Alfred Smee. 'My bullfinch loves his slice of apple, my horse thanks me in many little signs for the gift of an apple, and my cows delight to be offered one. The pigs, the chickens, the geese, all run to seize the windfalls as they drop, and sometimes get into the trees to procure the fruit.'

The natural ripening of the grape occurred at this season. In his account of a garden Charles Dudley

PORTUGAL QUINCE

Warner complained that the robin, 'the most knowing and greedy bird . . . has discovered that the grape-crop is uncommonly good, and has come back, with his whole tribe and family, larger than it was in pea-time. He knows the ripest bunches as well as anybody, and tries them all.'

In the flower garden the fragrance of summer has departed and in place of pinks and carnations are scentless dahlias, asters and Michaelmas daisies. As the leaves on the trees begin to turn, bringing a new sequence of colours into the garden, the chrysanthemum occupies pride of place. White, lemon-yellow, pink-purple, bronze, their blooms varying in size and compactness, they exude a healthy, peppery smell.

'Nature, who knows the most favourable moment to display her works', wrote William Howitt in his *Book of the Seasons*, 'has now instructed the spider to form its radiated circle on every bush, and the gossamer spider to hang its silken threads on every blade of grass.' This is the season for blackberrying and nutting, and for despoiling hives of their honey before the bees begin of necessity to consume the produce of their summer labours.

Sweeping and raking the fallen leaves from lawns and walks is now the order of the day, and the air is permeated with the smell of damp vegetation and the smoke from all the bonfires.

*My very heart faints and my whole*
*soul grieves*
*At the moist rich smell of the rotting*
*leaves,*
*And the breath*
*Of the fading edges of box beneath,*
*And the last year's rose.*
*Heavily hangs the broad sunflower*
*Over its groves i' the earth so chilly;*
*Heavily hangs the hollyhock,*
*Heavily hangs the tiger-lily.*

Tennyson

YELLOW AUTUMN RASPBERRY

COB NUT

November is generally a month of boisterous weather: 'the roaring of the woods and the rattling of branches, and the falling leaves, which are blown into dark and dreary places, are certain harbingers of winter', wrote Samuel Beeton.

It was at the beginning of the month that Rider Haggard visited the bulb sales in London, as recounted by him in *A Gardener's Year*. 'All kinds of buyers are gathered here, from the country nurseryman, who is taking thousands to retail, down to the City clerk, who has run in from his counting-house to secure a bag of Crocuses for his little suburban garden, or a few potting Hyacinths for his lean-to greenhouse.' He described the porters pushing their way through the crowd carrying the brown bags, releasing some of their contents on to the table for the inspection of intending bidders. The scene struck him as similar to that on his lawn when the starlings were in occupation.

COSFORD NUT

# DAHLIAS AND CHRYSANTHEMUMS

FOR A GOOD show of colour in the autumn the Victorian gardener's favourites were dahlias and chrysanthemums. Neither was native to the British Isles: the dahlia was discovered in Mexico in 1789; the chrysanthemum was introduced from China in the 1780s. Both species were transformed in England by the judicious attentions of nineteenth-century nurserymen.

By the 1830s the interest in dahlias was considerable, and competitions for the largest and most perfect blooms were held up and down the country. The exhibits, many of which would have been grown by cottagers, included doubles, compact pompon dahlias (known also as 'show' or 'fancy' dahlias) and cactus dahlias. Advising on the cultivation of prize blooms, W. D. Drury, in his *Book of Gardening*, recommended the use of cardboard caps to provide necessary shade from the sun and individual muslin bags as protection against troublesome thrips, and he reminded his readers of the importance of trapping earwigs. When showing chrysanthemums, a fine brush for dusting and a pair of ivory tweezers were indispensable for dressing the blooms and for curling and arranging the petals in the symmetrical manner approved by the judges.

'Queen of the Autumn' was the epithet employed by Mr Drury for the chrysanthemum, 'incomparable for a gorgeous display and wealth of colour'. Chrysanthemums for cutting were grown in pots under glass, supplying the house with flowers all through the autumn and winter.

# DAHLIAS AND CHRYSANTHEMUMS

*Thomas M'Kenzie's seed catalogue for 1886.*

# Button-holes and Bouquets

For ladies, 'hand-bouquets, breast or dress bouquets or sprays, wreaths, coronets, and sprays for the hair'; for gentlemen, 'button-hole bouquets and coat-flowers'; thus was the fashion for floral adornment described by F. W. Burbidge in *Domestic Floriculture.*

Bouquets were made from 'choice flowers, wires, lace-paper, or real lace

*A spray of flowers for the hair. Tiny reservoirs of water were often attached to both hair flowers and buttonholes so that the flowers did not wilt.*

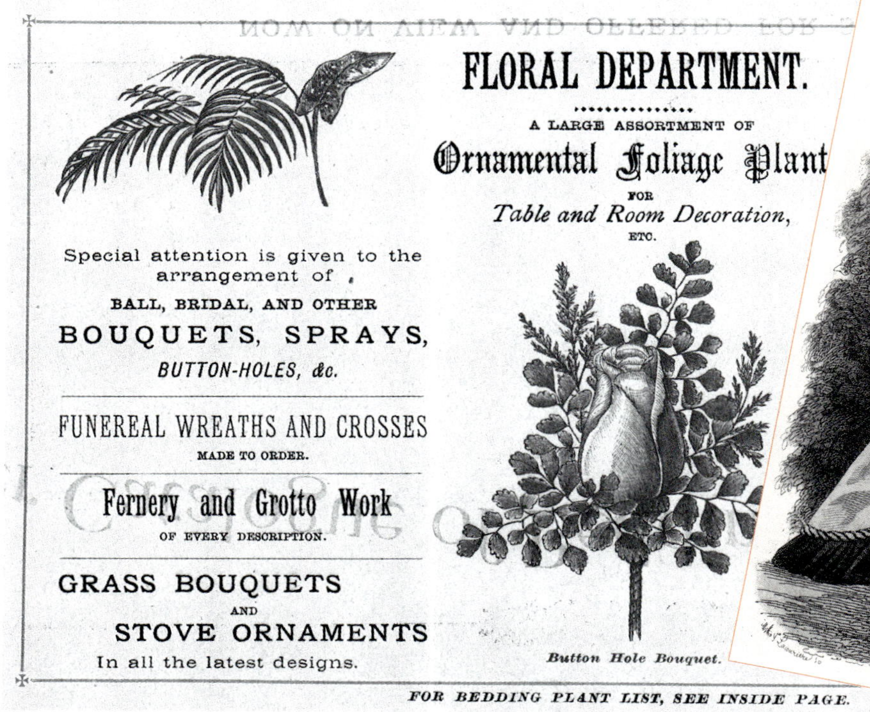

and ribbons of finest satin'. Basket-work holders could be obtained for transporting the flowers to the ball. For the hair, camellias, orchids, water lilies, lily of the valley, flowers of a 'thick fleshy character' that would survive the evening without water, were recommended.

The arrangements were bought from a florist or made at home, perhaps with the assistance of a maid. Competitions for children destined to go into service were held to give them practice in the art of flower arranging so that they might one day command a higher salary.

## BUTTON-HOLES AND BOUQUETS

Bouquet holder closed, with Bouquet in it

*'In a properly made bouquet the flowers are not crowded, and they are easily held by a small hand. In all cases the stem of the nosegay should be inserted into a metal bouquet-holder to prevent the glove being soiled by the damp.'* So instructed Robert Thompson in The Gardener's Assistant.

# Autumn Fruit

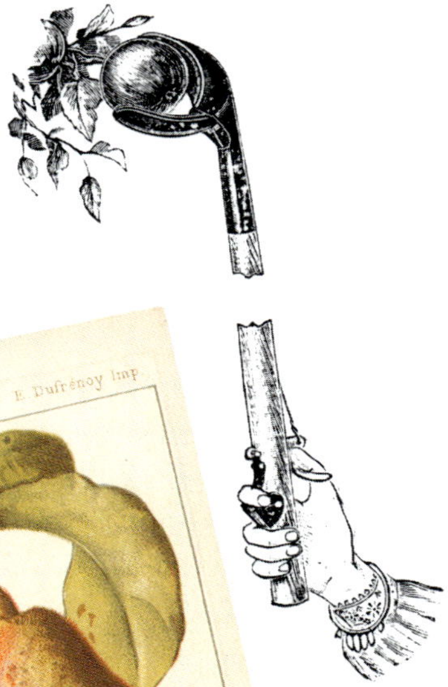

*Ankers Perfect Fruit Gatherer. 'A padding of soft felt inside the japanned jaws prevents any danger of bruising the fruits', it was available from the catalogue of W. B. Fordham & Sons of King's Cross.*

THE APPLE was universally allowed to be the most useful of fruits, and certainly no other was more extensively cultivated. As an eater or cooker, for immediate consumption or for storing or preserving, the apple was indispensable to every household, the fruit for gardens of all classes. Apple trees blossomed in May and generally escaped the frost that so often destroyed the crops of fruit trees such as the plum.

In *The Book of the Garden*, Charles M'Intosh included a list of 'Apples of excellent quality for a small garden in Britain, where twelve trees are only required, the climate being moderately good'; among them were the Keswick codlin, Herefordshire permain and Wormsley pippin.

Pear trees were particular favourites of the Victorians and also popular were the quince, the medlar and the apricot. The finest apricots that Mrs Loudon ever saw were growing on a tree trained against the wall of a cottage, the owner of which was an old woman who took in washing and was in the habit, nearly every day, of pouring down about the tree a quantity of soap-suds.

'Fruit gathering is one of the most cheerful and agreeable employments connected with garden management,' wrote Samuel Beeton. 'Several little contrivances have at different times been introduced to the public, in order to assist the fruit gatherer; but these, as far as they come under our own observation, are more remarkable for their neatness and ingenuity than for their general usefulness. Undoubtedly, the human hand is the best and safest of all fruit gatherers.'

*A reward of merit card given to good schoolchildren.*

# AUTUMN FRUIT

The medlar, the last fruit to ripen, 'has a peculiar flavour and acidulous taste, relished by some but disliked by others'.

'The Apple Gatherers' by Frederick Morgan (below).

A plate from Loudon's The Horticulturist.

Boxes for fruit packing. 'Each fruit is contained in a wooden cylinder.'

## Composts and Manures

*So popular was Peruvian guano that Robert Thompson wrote in 1878, 'considerable uneasiness has been caused in this country lest the beds of guano become exhausted'. This led to the discovery of alternative deposits in south-west Africa and the Arabian Gulf.*

EVERY GARDENER knew that successful cultivation depended in part on giving back to the soil what was taken from it by plants. Among the composts listed by Robert Thompson in *The Gardener's Assistant: Practical and Scientific* were horse, cow and pig dung and night-soil; peat, sawdust, rape-dust, malt-dust (obtained from the brewer); ox blood, fish, bone (invaluable for turnips) and granules of blubber (very satisfactory results with peas, beans and potatoes). In Kent, Berkshire and Oxfordshire woollen rags were much employed. His list of inorganic manures included the ammoniacal liquor waste from gas manufacture, which had notable results in improving lawns.

The miracle manure of the age was guano, the dried excrement of sea birds. Care had to be taken not to use too concentrated a solution as this had the opposite effect to what was desired. Guano began to arrive by the shipload from the Pacific islands – notably the three Chinca Islands – in the 1840s. It was marketed under such names as Canary and Icthemic.

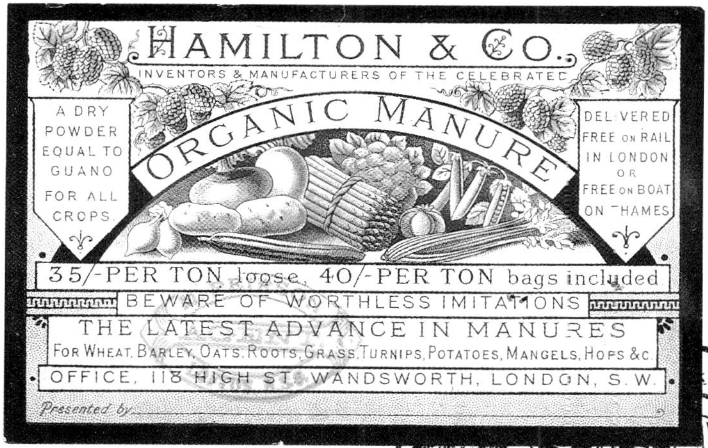


# COMPOSTS AND MANURES

Measurement of Dung at Cairnie sold by Mr.
James Ranken to Capt. Hope R.N.
Y F I
162 : 13 . 6 — at 2/- per yard
Septr 23 Settled James Ranken
Musselburgh 29 March 1836

*All manner of plant foods and composts were introduced in the wake of the success of guano, but many people still relied on farmyard manure.*

# FERNS AND FERNERIES

*'The Fern Gatherer' by C. S. Lidderdale (bottom left).*

The passion for ferns, 'pteridomania' in contemporary parlance, lasted from the 1850s to the end of the 1870s. Fern hunters sent to each corner of the globe for new specimens and searched every rocky crevice in Britain, aided in their quest by the new and spreading railway network.

*Ferns flourished in the moist confinement of Wardian cases. They would be planted in peat mixed with soft charcoal, silver sand and leaf mould.*

Shirley Hibberd recommended beginning with a small outdoor fernery: a little bracken bought from an itinerant vendor and grown on a pile of broken hearth stone. But he also proposed far more grandiose creations with 'plumy emerald pets glistening with health and beadings of warm dew': a grand fernery with a model ruin composed in a manner representing the mountain dells, ancestral beeches and ancient banks above water-brooks that trickle from unseen founts of the ferns' natural habitat.

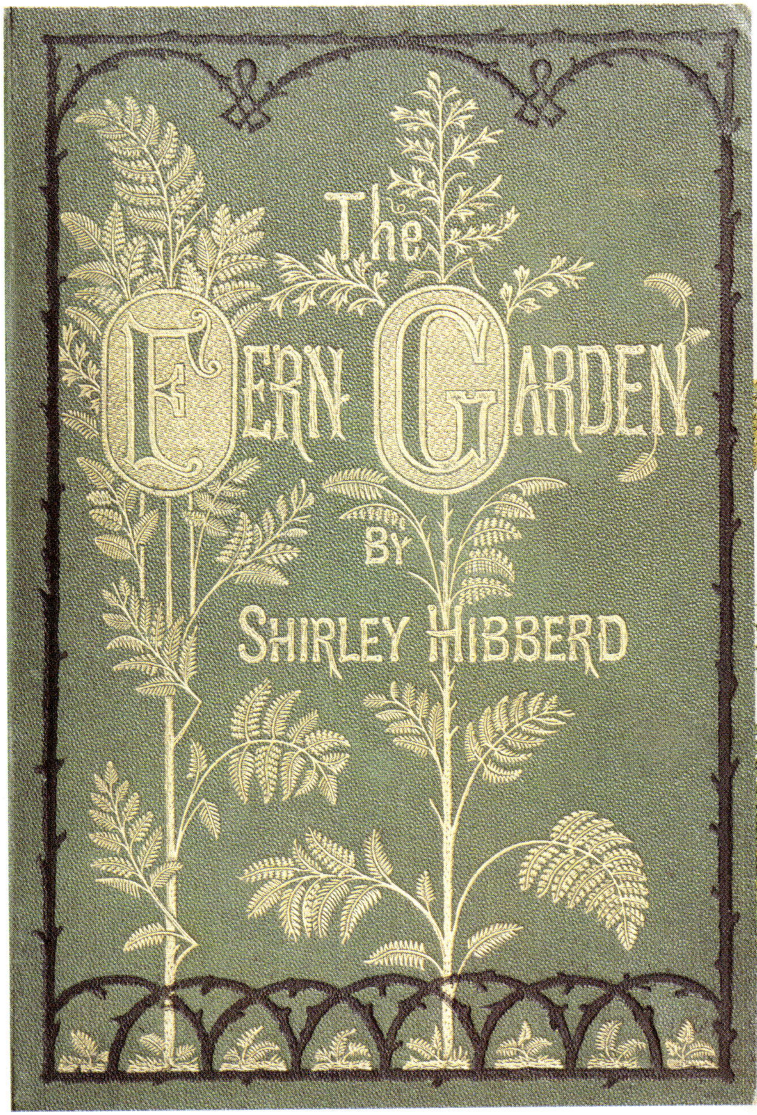

*In his book for beginners in fern culture, Hibberd included chapters on the fernery at the fireside, the art of multiplying ferns, gold and silver ferns and thirty select stove ferns.*

# PARLOUR GARDENING

*'Those who possess conservatories and greenhouses can always bring tender plants into the house for decorative purposes, removing them again when they have done flowering or are showing signs of exhaustion', wrote F. W. Burbidge, who illustrated the portable ivy screen (below) and the sofa arbour (far right) amidst yuccas, New Zealand flax, palms and India rubber plants.*

THE WARDIAN CASE, AND WINTER GARDEN.

IN princely halls, and courts of kings,
Its lustrous ray the diamond flings,
Yet few of those who see its beams,
Amid the torchlight's dazzling gleams,
As bright as though a meteor shone,
Can call the costly prize their own;
But gems of every form and hue
Are glittering here in morning dew;
Jewels that all alike may share
As freely as the common air.

CHAPTER I.

OW common to us all is the love of greenness and flowery life! How the peer rejoices in his spacious park, and the peasant in his little garden! How tenderly the pretty belles assort the cut-flowers for the boudoir



*A page from Shirley Hibberd's* Rustic Adornments.

THE NOTION that plants exuded noxious gases in the hours of darkness was discussed and dispelled during the course of the nineteenth century; and, perhaps because every flower 'compels us to cherish thoughts of purity and images of peace,' according to Shirley Hibberd, 'whatever can be done to render their culture easy, and to bring them to perfection in the vicinity or within the household, must be regarded as a benefaction'. There was one way of preserving real verdure indoors 'in the freshness of its original strength and life, and that is by the culture of it in Wardian Cases'.

Invented by Nathaniel B. Ward in 1829, the cases served originally to create a closed, unchanging atmosphere in which to transport plants on

A *Wardian case of ferns.*

lengthy journeys. In the home, they became 'nothing more or less than a greenhouse on a small scale'. The most suitable occupants of the cases were ferns; though protected by the glass from the smoke and soot of coal fires and oil and gas lamps, flowering plants were on the whole to be exhibited rather than grown in the cases.

Hanging baskets of plants, including ivy, were suggested for decorating the parlour by F. W. Burbidge. He revealed that in Paris, America, northern Germany and Russia, ivy was 'trained over portable screens, and even couches or sofas are overshadowed by a fresh green bower of its bright glossy leaves'.



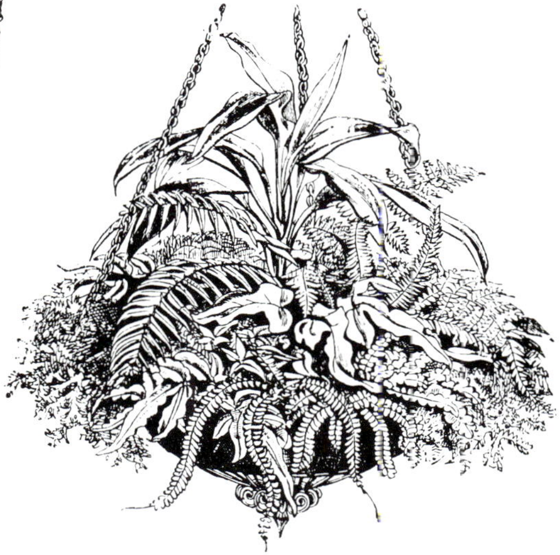

*Rosher's Fern Pillar: an elaborate planter for growing ferns inside a glazed case.*

# HARVEST

*Sheaves of corn, festoons of Virginia creeper and ivy, bunches of grapes and apples and flowers from the garden decorated the church at Harvest Festival.*

THANKSGIVING for the harvest was celebrated in September, when all the corn was gathered in and the apples were ripening on the trees.

On 15 September 1870 the Rev. Francis Kilvert recorded in his diary, 'We were busy all day dressing the Church or preparing decorations. Mrs Price and Miss Elcox had got a quantity of wild hops from the fields and were arranging bright apples for ornament. Also they had boughs loaded with rosy apples and quantities of bright yellow Siberian crabs. At the school the children were busy leasing out corn from a loose heap on the floor, sitting among the straw and tying up wheat, barley and oats in small sheaves and bundles.' The window-sills were decorated with flowers, and fruit and ferns were brought for the chancel. The font was dressed with moss and white asters under the sweeping fronds of a silver fern, and round the base 'were twined the delicate light green sprays of white convolvulus'.

'It is well to be careful in the use of yellow flowers,' warned F. W. Burbidge, 'as many of these have a glaring or gaudy appearance, not in keeping with the quiet rich softness of colouring and peaceful harmony of arrangement which should at all times prevail within a sacred edifice.'

# HARVEST

*A harvest trophy (below) and other images of rural plenty including an American advertising card (left).*

# DRIED FLOWERS

AGREEABLE as a pastime was the mounting of dried flowers, grasses and autumn leaves of varied brown and deep red hues as greeting cards, or on screens that would provide ornament for the fireplace in summer. Skeletonized leaves of the sycamore, poplar and willow, created

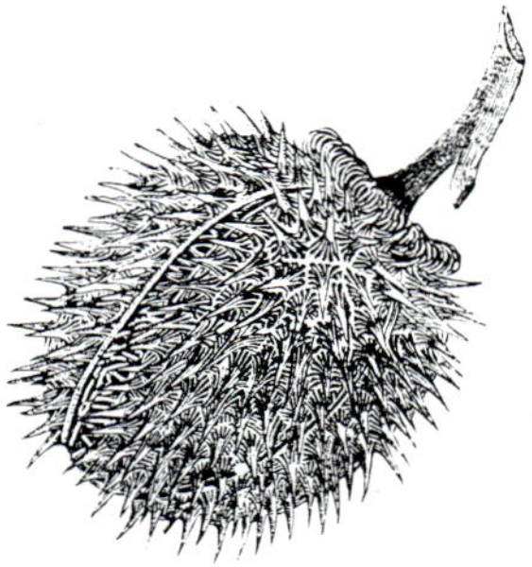

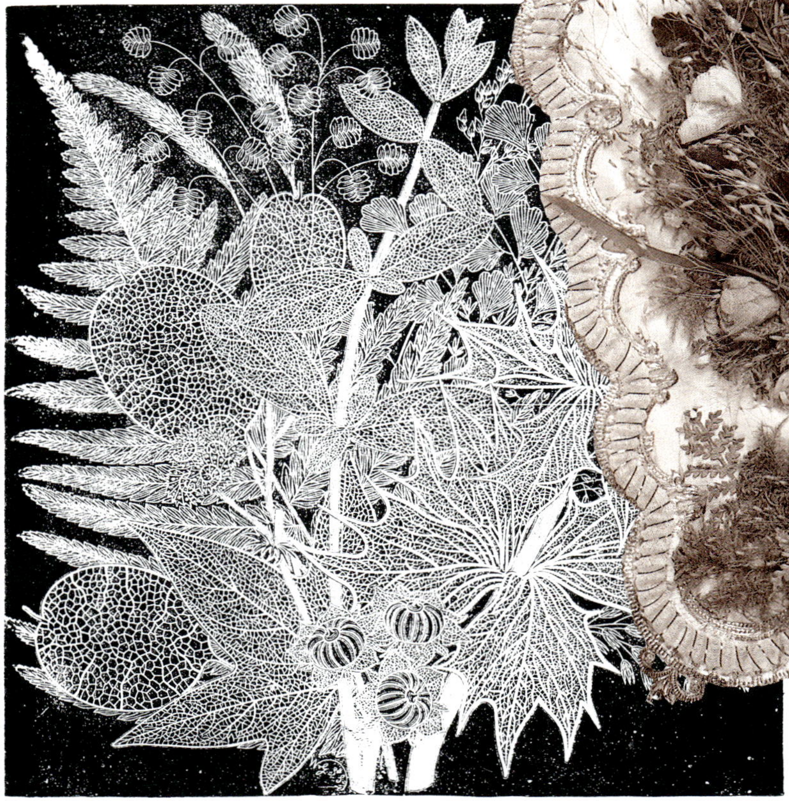

*Skeleton leaves, an arrangement suitable for a firescreen (right); valentine of dried grasses and scraps of material (far right).*

by the process of maceration, made exquisite decoration. Everlasting flowers, dried seed pods and grasses were arranged in vases for the mantelpiece, and in baskets for the drawing-room and parlour table; glass domes were placed over them so as to prevent any dust from settling on the arrangement.

## Dried Flowers

*Advertisement for commercially dried leaves, 'Every Leaf Prettier than Another' (far left); printed card with dried flowers, leaves and grasses (left).*

*Skeleton leaves from* The Popular Recreator.

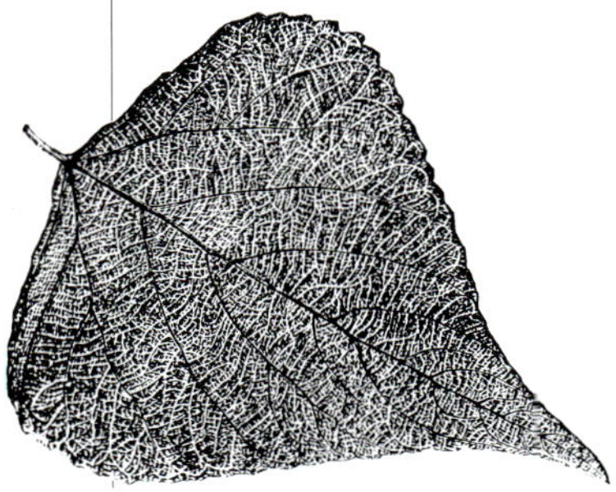

## DECEMBER

**VEGETABLES.** – The work to be performed this month will, in many respects, be similar to last month. In favourable weather, continue to trench, dig, and manure all vacant ground, leaving a rough surface, as formerly recommended. Take advantage of frosty weather to wheel or collect manure to spots intended for spring cropping. Make another sowing of early peas and beans on a sheltered situation. Plant a few kidney-shaped potatoes on a sheltered border; protect them with litter if frost sets in. If required, sea-kale and rhubarb may be forced in the open ground; put tall pots over the crowns, covering them with stable litter or leaves to keep up a gentle heat.

**FLOWERS.** – Cover hyacinth and tulip beds with mats or other covering to protect from frost, and give protection to flowering shrubs, roses, etc., not thoroughly hardy; remove the covering in mild sunny days. In mild weather transplant trees, flowering shrubs, roses, etc. Lay off flower beds, and carry out any necessary ground alterations in favourable weather. Look over plants housed for stock, and give attention as recommended last month.

**FRUITS.** – Continue to look over all stored fruit, as formerly recommended; admit plenty of air to the room in mild weather. Prune gooseberries, currants, and fruit trees in the open ground; also prune and train wall fruit trees. In mild weather transplant hardy fruit trees, but not too deep.

## JANUARY

**VEGETABLES.** – Sow Daniel O'Rourke peas and Mazagan beans in a sheltered situation; protect from frost those sown in autumn by inserting spruce twigs along each side of the rows. Plant early York and Nonpareil cabbages; also Ash-leaf Kidney or other early potatoes in warm borders. In dry, open weather, trench and turn up all spare ground, leaving a rough surface exposed to the action of the elements. In frosty weather collect manure to plots intended for cropping. Prepare hot-beds for forcing early vegetables.

**FLOWERS.** – Protect from frost, hyacinths, tulips, anemones, and ranunculuses, planted in autumn. Transplant roses, and mulch them with a few inches of short dung. Protect from frost tender ever-greens and flowering shrubs. Plant anemones and ranunculus. Sow sweet peas for early flowering. Dig vacant flower plots as required for vegetables.

**FRUITS.** – Examine stored fruit, and remove any that shows signs of decay. In open, mild weather, all kinds of fruit trees may be transplanted; care should be taken not to plant too deep, or in a richly-manured soil. Apples, pears, and plums, will be found more prolific when planted in soil of medium quality. In fine weather prune and train wall fruit trees; finish pruning currants, gooseberries, and raspberries; fork in a dressing of well-rotted manure round the bushes.

## FEBRUARY

**VEGETABLES.** – Sow, if the weather permits, in warm, sheltered places, early and second-early peas, long-pod beans, and look to the protection of earlier sown crops. Towards the end of the month make small sowings of early cabbage, onions, leeks, parsnips, parsley, early turnips, lettuce, spinage, radish, mustard, and cress. In suitable weather transplant Nonpareil, Enfield Market, and Drumhead cabbages from the autumn sowings, also a few Red Dutch for pickling.

**FLOWERS.** – Protect from frost all autumn-planted bulbs and early flowering plants. Finish planting anemones and ranunculus early in the month. Gladioli may be planted in pots, and kept in a cold frame till the severe frosts are over, when they should be planted in their permanent quarters. Plant daisies, auriculas, primroses, polyanthus, and other spring-flowering plants. Propagate herbaceous plants by dividing the roots. Trim box-edgings, and fill up vacant spots. Sow hardy annuals in pans to succeed those sown in autumn.

**FRUITS.** – Continue planting, pruning, and training in suitable weather. Recently-planted trees should be trenched with a few inches of short dung. Protect from frost the flower buds of wall fruit trees with spruce twigs, Frigi domo, Tiffany, or other suitable covering. Fork in a dressing of well-rotted manure about the roots of wall fruit trees and those in the open ground. Plant cuttings of approved varieties of gooseberries and currants.

WINTER

WINTER

LAUREL

# WINTER

THE EVERGREEN trees 'with their beautiful cones, such as firs and pines, are now particularly observed and valued; the different species of everlasting flowers, so pleasing an ornament to our parlours in winter, and indeed during the whole year, also attract our attention. The oak, the beech and the hornbeam, in part retain their leaves, while all other trees are entirely denuded. The scarlet berries of the holly, and the fiery bunches of Pyracantha on its dark green, thorny sprays, are brightly conspicuous, and the mosses are in their pride', wrote William Howitt in *The Book of the Seasons*.

At Christmas holly, mistletoe and ivy were used to decorate the house and church. Ivy would insinuate itself into every crevice, passing through hinges and even the floors of outbuildings, and, when it had nothing to which it could conveniently cling, would hang down in wild festoons as if predestined for a decorative purpose.

WINTER FLOWERS

For Dean Hole winter was an active time of year. 'Then you superintended the arrangement of your small winter garden, the Thujas, Acubas, Gold and Silver Hollies, Arabis, Ivies and Heaths, which you keep in pots . . . having looked into your fruit-room, and counted, like a miser, your golden store; having glanced with a paternal pride over your numerous progeny of nursery stock, the rising generation of dandies and belles, who are to rule the beau-monde next year, you went into your vinery, and cut those grand bunches of Muscats and Hamburghs, which not only made you a dessert fit for an emperor, but, taken in part to a sick neighbour, brought you a far greater luxury – "the luxury of doing good".'

The vinery, orchid house and other glasshouses heated to an unseasonable temperature afforded a pleasant contrast to the barren aspect of the garden. Not only grapes but pineapples and strawberries would be produced for the dessert on Christmas Day, and exquisitely scented lilac for table decoration.

Breaking the somnolence in the garden was the winter jasmine and

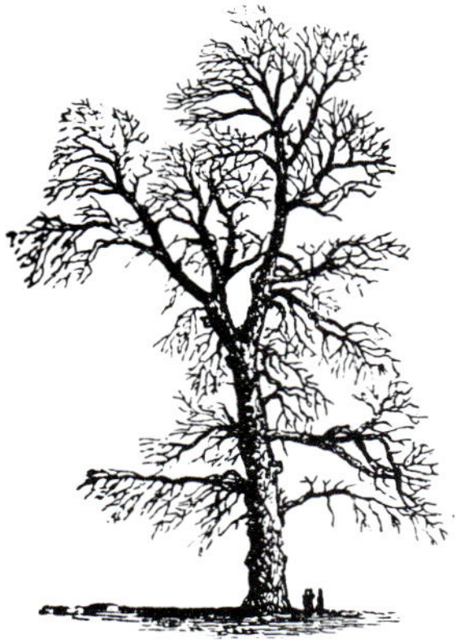

Old black poplar

the wych-hazel, most favoured of the winter-flowering shrubs, its branches bursting into yellow life. There might be a glimpse, too, of the Christmas rose, glorified in a northern setting by Anne Brontë in *The Tenant of Wildfell Hall*: 'This Rose is not so fragrant as a summer flower, but it has stood through hardships none of them could bear: the cold rain of winter has sufficed to nourish it, and its faint sun to warm it; the bleak winds have not blanched it, or broken its stem, and the keen frost has not blighted it.'

In the first days of January, Rider Haggard wrote in *A Gardener's Year*, 'I gather this morning a white Rose-bud and a single flower of Anemone that is whiter yet. To me the one is as a ghost from the grave of dead, forgotten Summer and the other a spirit of the Spring, breathing that eternal promise which was from the ancient days and evermore shall be.'

Much of the business of the garden now consisted in matting and defending plants against the cold and preparing the earth for spring, trenching and turning up the soil and manuring. Herbaceous plants were divided and, in the kitchen garden, the first sowings were made of onions, parsnips, peas and beans.

During mild weather, 'slugs are in constant motion, preying on plants,' wrote William Howitt. 'Their coverings of slime prevent the escape of animal heat, and hence they are enabled to ravage when their brethren of the shell are compelled to be dormant. Earth-worms, likewise, appear about this time, but let not the man of nice order be too precipitate in destroying *them* – they are the under-gardeners that loosen the subsoil, and have their uses in conveying away superfluous moisture, and admitting a supply of air to the roots of plants.'

Cedars of Lebanon and evergreen oak

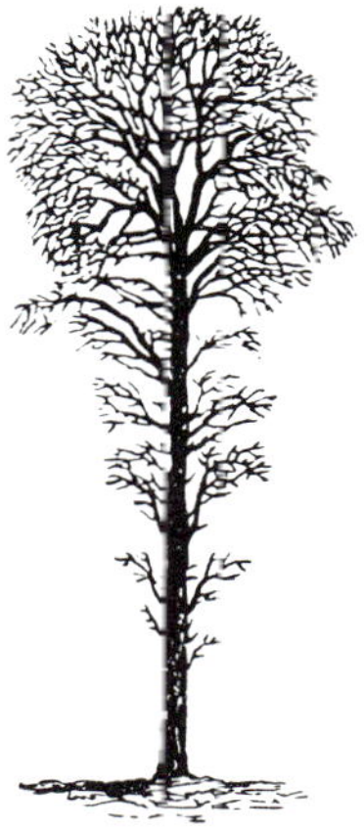

White poplar

## Winter

Holly

# EXOTICS FROM THE TROPICS

With the 'permanent summer' that could be simulated in a glasshouse, 'An inexhaustible fund of novelty seems to be in store for us', declared James Bateman. In *Orchidaceae of Mexico and Guatemala* he recounted the sacrifices made by the redoubtable

*Calanthea Veitcheii, from tropical America, with the richly marked and brightly coloured foliage for which many stove plants were prized.*

Mr Skinner, and the hardships he had suffered – 'whether detained in quarantine on the shores of the Atlantic or shipwrecked on the rocks of the Pacific' – in order to add to his array of botanical discoveries.

In far-distant parts of the globe Victorian plant hunters sought out and sent home exotic plants; gloxinia, amaryllis and achimenes from South America, poinsettia and tydaea from Mexico, dracaena from Madagascar. The exact degree of heat and moisture required by the various orchids was known and could be achieved. Robert Thompson wrote, 'it is a wonderful feat that we are able to collect plants from such different climes and such varied situations, and succeed so well with them'.

The glasshouses heated to high temperatures for the exotics were known as 'stoves', and the most satisfactory structures had span roofs which encouraged growth by letting in as much light as possible. 'In the arrangement of Stove plants,' wrote George Nicholson in the *Illustrated Dictionary of Gardening*, 'overcrowding should be avoided as growth is rapid with many of them, and the plants soon become drawn or one-sided. Cleanliness amongst plants, and also pots, is of great importance: a high Stove temperature favours the multiplication of insects.'

*Frontispiece to* The Flower Garden *by C. M'Intosh, in which he announced a subsequent volume on tender and exotic plants.*

*A manufacturer's label.*

# THE CONSERVATORY

*A gentleman in his conservatory, painted by a follower of Tissot.*

*Coloured plates from* The Amateur's Greenhouse and Conservatory, *1883, by Shirley Hibberd.*

THE 'GARDEN under glass' was an extension of the Victorian drawing room. John Loudon was of the opinion that conservatories were desirable additions to the house 'as indicating the residence of ease and elegance; as affording a useful source of exercise and recreation in severe weather, and in winter'. Shirley Hibberd agreed, remarking that 'above all things, the conservatory should be attractive in the dull months of the year'. He also noted that 'its occupants should not be such as require a high temperature, for it is not well to take a vapour bath every time the mind desires refreshment in the midst of vegetable beauty.'

An atmosphere of romantic exoticism in the conservatory was described by the novelist G. J. Whyte-Melville

Bouvardia longiflora

in *The White Rose*. 'There side by side, gathered from the far east and the far west, blossomed and reigned Nature's most regal flower daughters. Gorgeous stately flowers, that had hitherto revealed their passionate hearts, fold after fold, to the fainting air of some cloudless, rainless, brazen, tropic sky, now poured forth all their sweets, put on all their brilliant apparel.'

# The Conservatory

*A photograph of the steps from a house to its conservatory (above). 'The Bunch of Lilacs' (right), a painting by James Tissot.*

# HOTHOUSE FRUIT

*Charlotte Rothschild pineapple, engraved in* The Gardener's Assistant *which describes it as 'flesh yellow, very juicy, flavour excellent when ripened in high temperature . . . especially valuable as winter fruit'.*

MELONS, apricots, peaches and nectarines, figs, grapes, strawberries and pineapples: with the aid of glasshouses, powerful boilers and forcing pits and beds all these could be produced in winter and provide a sumptuous display of fruit for Christmas.

Fruit and vegetables to be forced were planted on a hotbed composed of fermenting matter – usually dung – and grown under glass. Robert Thompson, concerned in *The Practical Gardener* with the forcing of melons, analysed the heat achieved by different materials: 'sheep's dung lasts four months giving heat of 141° to 158°; the dung of the horse, mule or ass, six months, affording a temperature of 122° to 140°; dung of horned cattle, eight months, producing a heat of 95° to 113°; but if it is mixed with the dung of pigeons or poultry a higher temperature may be obtained. Tan lasts six months, and dead leaves one year, giving in each case a heat of 95° to 104°.' He described scarlet-, white- and green-fleshed melons, all with names that bore testimony to their place of breeding: Eastnor Castle, Trentham Hybrid, Bromham Hall.

Alfred Smee produced grapes in his Surrey hothouse all the year round. On New Year's Eve 1870,

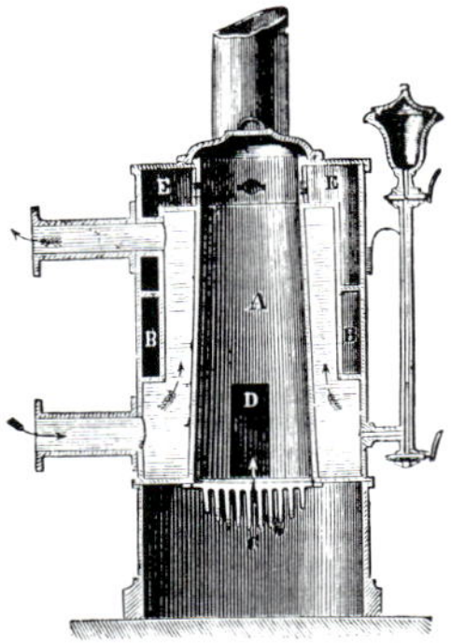



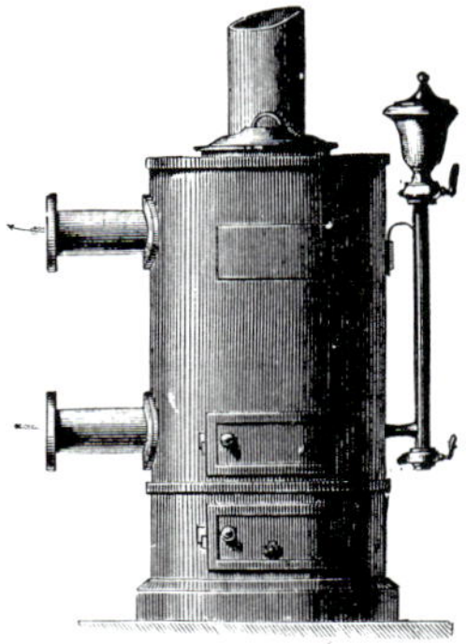

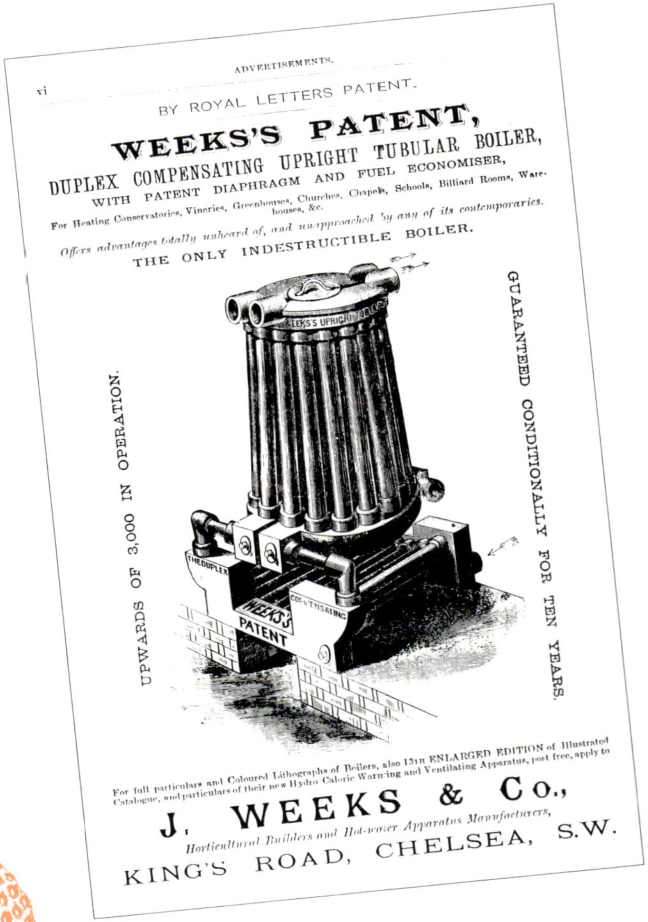

*The boilers sold by J. Weeks & Co. were the most reliable of the period, and enabled such fruit as Laxton's Noble strawberry to be grown in winter.*

when his garden had a deep covering of snow, he recorded: 'Our vinery was well supplied with grapes. Lady Downe's and West's St. Peter's were scarcely in perfection. Ingram's Prolific Muscat and Snow's Muscat Hamburgh were excellent; the Black Hamburgh and Buckland's Sweetwater were rather past; but the White Tokay, Canon Hall, Muscat of Alexandria, and Bowood Muscat were perfectly good and hanging upon the trees.'

It was not only the grapes that benefited from the temperature in the hothouse. 'The cats had found out the warmth of the glass and delighted to sit upon it.'

*The black grapes are Lady Downe's Seedling (left) and the white ones White Tokay (below).*

## HOTHOUSE FRUIT

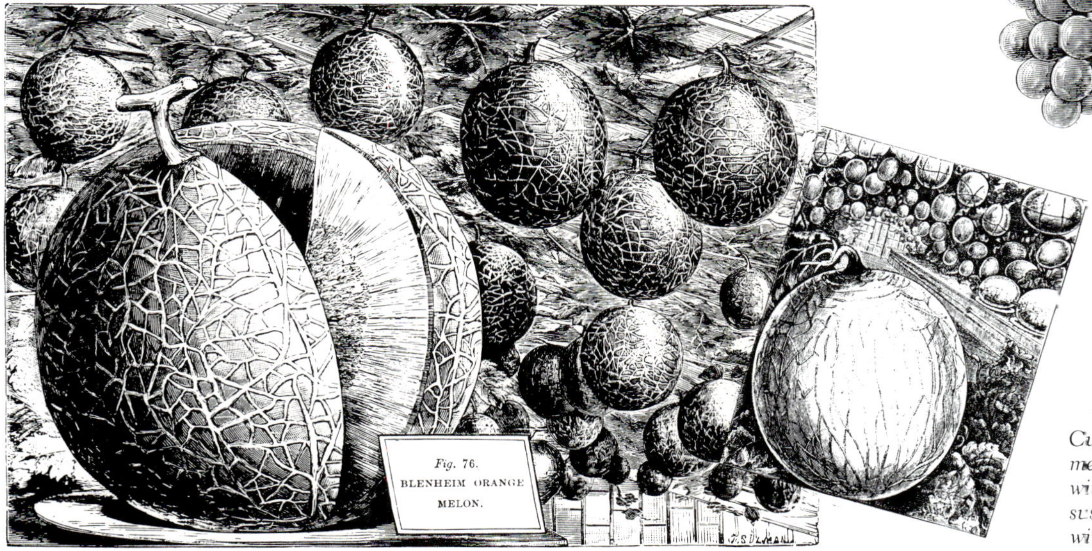


*Cucumbers and melons were grown with vines, suspended from wires.*

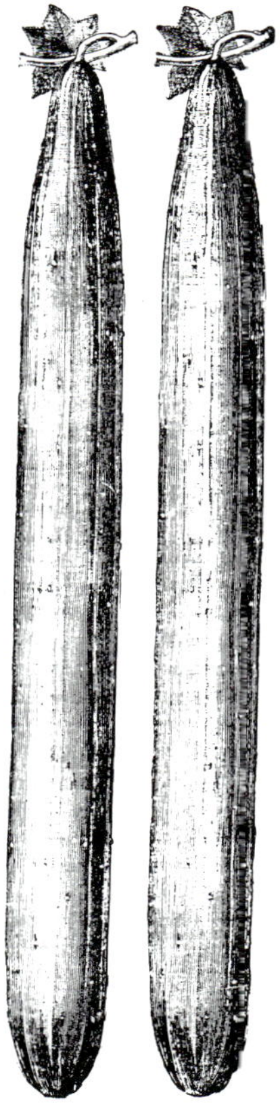

# GAMES WITH FLOWERS

FLOWER-LOVERS found winter diversion in a variety of delightful games. With *The Realm of the Queen of Flowers*, proclaimed as a 'Rational Entertainment', the players would compose an arrangement of engraved and coloured flowers in a vase. Each type of flower symbolized its own message in the Language of Flowers; a camellia, for instance, conveyed the following sentiment: 'I hold thee for an angel fair/ If not, the stars speak false'. The completed composition, put together with taste and elegance, would 'serve as a model

for drawing and painting, and even for embroidery.'

Another game, called *Floral Loto*, served to inform as well as entertain. It was designed, claimed the manufacturer John Jaques, to 'encourage in young persons a love of flowers, and impart, by the agency of cheerful recreation, a knowledge of their names, both English and botanical, together with the emblematic sentiments which they are supposed to convey'. Thus the Crocus, *Crocus Vernus*, stood for Youthfulness; the Tulip, *Tulipa Gesneriana*, for a Declaration of Love.

# Gardening Books

*These two books, both published the year Queen Victoria died, demonstrate the growing diversity of garden literature.*

The Victorians' ever-increasing passion for gardening was matched with a proliferation of publications. There were now more houses, more gardens and, thanks to improved methods of printing, many more books.

One of the most conscientious garden writers was John Claudius Loudon, to whom was owed an indispensable encyclopedia of gardening. His sister Jane was the author of A *Treatise on Insects Injurious to Gardeners*, and his wife (also called Jane) had a prodigious success with *Practical Instructions in Gardening for Ladies*, which, between 1841 and 1879, ran to nine editions. Her later books on ornamental annuals, perennials, bulbous and greenhouse plants were all addressed to ladies.

Shirley Hibberd directed most of his books to the amateur, covering all matters from the frame ground and forcing pit to the rose garden. Both Loudon and Hibberd perceived town and suburban dwellers as a new market, Loudon publishing *The Suburban Gardener and Villa Companion* and Hibberd *The Town Garden*. Mrs Haweis, best known for her books on interior decoration, was the author of *Rus in Urbe: or Flowers that Thrive in London Gardens and Smoky Towns*. The problems of those possessed of nothing greater than a window ledge were considered in John Mollison's *The New Practical Window Gardener*.

Writers who had the authority of experience, particularly regarding the management of extensive gardens, were Charles M'Intosh, 'Gardener to His Majesty the King of the Belgians at Claremont', and H. W. Ward, the Earl of Radnor's head gardener. Ward's *My Gardener: A Practical Handbook for the Million* was addressed particularly to his lordship's tenants.

*Two garden lover's book plates and the fifth edition of* One & All Gardening.

# CHRISTMAS

Scrap of a Victorian child bringing home the Christmas tree.

MANY of the customs attaching to Christmas were introduced during Queen Victoria's reign, among them that of sending Christmas cards. Pictured on the cards were children bearing home the holly and mistletoe and bringing in the Yule log. Snowdrops, scillas and white Christmas roses – flowers that braved the winter frosts and snow – represented another favourite theme.

*Scillas were regarded by William Robinson as indispensable garden flowers. They bloomed in winter and on into the spring.*

# CHRISTMAS

The Christmas tree, introduced from Germany, was made popular by Prince Albert. For decorating the tree, Mrs Valentine, author of *The Home Book of Pleasure and Instruction*, recommended hanging small garlands or bunches of crystallized leaves from the branches. Her instructions for covering the green twigs with crystals were to take the lightest sprays of spruce, fir, or box and 'suspend them by a network of string tied across the top of a deep bucket, into which they must hang. Then put into the bucket a pound of alum, and pour a gallon of boiling water on it. Leave it all night untouched. Remove the twigs carefully the next morning, and you will find them glittering with minute crystals resembling diamonds.' The twigs were then ready for making up into festive ornaments.

Charles Dickens, in *Household Words*, described a Christmas tree placed in the middle of a great round table, lit by a multitude of tapers and laden with trinkets and bright objects: 'there were teetotums, humming tops, needle-cases, pen-wipers, smelling-bottles, conversation-cards, bouquet holders; real fruit made artificially dazzling with gold leaf; imitation apples, pears and walnuts crammed with surprises.' There was, in short, 'everything, and more'.

*The Christmas rose, with its white flowers and leathery pale green leaves, was grown out of doors and as a favourite pot plant.*

# HOLLY, IVY AND MISTLETOE

*The author of* Domestic Floriculture *suggested that it was 'no longer sufficient to fill the ancient font with an armful of holly and ivy.'*

THE DAY before Christmas all were employed in decorating the church. 'They had made some pretty ivy knots and branches for the pulpit panels and the ivy blossoms cleverly whitened with flour looked just like white flowers', wrote the Rev. Francis Kilvert. There were also wreaths of evergreen and clusters of white dried flowers with scarlet holly berries.

Arriving at the church porch on Christmas Day, 'we found the parson rebuking the grey-headed sexton for having used mistletoe among the greens with which the church was decorated', wrote Mary Howitt in her *Pictorial Calendar of the Seasons.* It was, the parson observed, 'an unholy plant, profaned by having been used by the Druids in their mystic ceremonies.' Though the mistletoe might be innocently employed in the ornamenting of halls and kitchens, so unfit for sacred purposes did he deem it that 'the poor sexton was obliged to strip down a great part of the humble trophies of his taste before the parson would consent to enter upon the service of the day'.

# Holly, Ivy and Mistletoe

*Festive designs made of holly.*

*Ivy twining round a hyacinth grown in a bulb glass.*

Most of the illustrations in *The Victorian Garden Album* (with the exception of the paintings) come under the category of ephemera. Ephemera is defined as the 'minor transient documents of every-day life': the sort of things which were not intended to be kept but, by amazing luck, have been rescued from dustbins, survived in attics and cupboards or been found between the pages of books. The ephemera shown on these two pages are chromolithographed and embossed floral scraps, which were used by the Victorians to decorate greeting cards and screens, and were also collected in albums. Most of the early ones – covering every imaginable subject, from travel to religion and, of course, including flowers – were produced in Germany. Their arrival in Britain dates from *c.* 1865 and the scraps were sold in sheets containing up to a dozen images. They could be purchased from stationers and originally cost 1d per sheet.

Ephemera is an area of collecting which is being increasingly recognized as providing an important link with the past. Bits of ephemera in isolation may be of limited interest, but when the finder or collector pieces together all the fragments available on a certain period or subject, they can provide a portrait of another time. As this album shows, the ephemera from the Victorian era includes a great variety of material on gardening, from greeting cards and seed catalogues to library lists and wage sheets.

Two world wars, the break up of large houses and the growing mobility of people's lifestyles have all contributed to a great deal of ephemera being lost or destroyed during this century. A fair amount, however, has survived and if you come across a nineteenth-century butcher's bill, a wine list from the 1930s or an invitation to attend the coronation of William IV, be sure to keep it. Although it is unlikely to possess anything other than a very modest monetary worth,

## ABOUT EPHEMERA

it could easily be invaluable to the social historian and it might start you collecting or be of interest to your local museum or school.

If you require specific advice or simply want more information on the subject please write to the Ephemera Society (with a stamped, addressed envelope). Founded in London in 1975, its success has led to other ephemera societies being set up in America, Canada and Australia. In 1993 the world's first Centre for Ephemera Studies opened at the University of Reading, England. Its aim is to encourage the use of printed throwaways as material for the study of social and printing history.

*The addresses of the various ephemera societies are as follows:*

*The Ephemera Society, 84 Marylebone High Street, London W1M 3DE*

*The Ephemera Society of America Inc., P. O. Box 10, Schoharie, NY 12157*

*The Ephemera Society of Canada Inc., 36 Macauley Drive, Thornhill, Ontario, L3T 5S5*

*The Ephemera Society of Australia Inc., P. O. Box 479, Warraguil, Victoria 3820*

# ACKNOWLEDGEMENTS

The ephemera reproduced in this book is from the collection of Amoret Tanner, to whom Elizabeth Drury and Philippa Lewis are extremely grateful. Paintings on the following pages are reproduced from the Bridgeman Art Library: 54, 62 (Cheltenham Museum & Art Gallery), 77, 97, 100, 115; and from Christie's Images: 76, 114.

Other illustrations, and quotations in the text, are from the following books: Barron, Archibald F., *Vines and Vine Culture* (London, 1887); *Beeton's Gardening Book* (London, n.d.); Beeton, S. O., *The Book of Garden Management* (London, 1862); Biddle, Violet P., *Small Gardens and how to make the most of them* (London, n.d.); Bright, Henry A., *A Year in a Lancashire Garden* (London, 1891); Burbidge, F. W., *Domestic Floriculture* (London, 1874); Cobbett, Anne, *The English Housekeeper* (London, 1842); Cook, E. T., *Gardens of England* (London, 1908); Drury, W. D., (ed.), *The Book of Gardening* (London, 1900); Haggard, H. Rider, *A Gardener's Year* (London, 1905); Haweis, Mrs, *Rus in Urbe* (London, 1886); Hibberd, Shirley, *The Amateur's Flower Garden* (London, 1878); Hibberd, Shirley, *The Amateur's Greenhouse and Conservatory* (London, 1883); Hibberd, Shirley, *The Amateur's Rose Book* (London, 1878); Hibberd, Shirley, *The Fern Garden* (London, 1872); Hibberd, Shirley, *Rustic Adornments for Homes of Taste* (London, 1870); Hibberd, Shirley, *The Town Garden* (London, 1859); Hobday, E., *Cottage Gardening* (London, 1877); Hole, S. Reynolds, *A Book about the Garden and the Gardener* (London, Edinburgh, Dublin and New York, 1909); Hole, S. Reynolds, *A Book about Roses* (Edinburgh and London, 1869); Howitt, Mary, *Pictorial Calendar of the Seasons* (London, 1854); Howitt, William, *The Book of the Seasons* (London, 1840); Johns, Rev. C. A., *Gardening for Children* (London, 1848); *Kilvert's Diary: 1870-1879* (ed. William Plomer; London, 1944); Loudon, Jane, *Gardening for Ladies* (London, 1841); Loudon, Jane, *The Country Lady's Companion* (London, 1845); Loudon, Jane, *My Own Garden* (London, 1855); Loudon, J. C., *The Horticulturist* (ed. and rev. William Robinson; London and New York, 1871); Loudon, J. C., *An Encyclopaedia of Cottage, Farm and Villa Architecture* (London, 1857); Maling, E. A., *Indoor Plants and How to Grow Them* (London, 1861); Meikle, Andrew, *The Cottage Garden* (London, 1874); Meikle, Andrew, *Window Gardening in Town and Country* (London and New York, 1879); Mintorn, Mrs J. H., *The Hand-book of Paper-flower Making* (London, 1870); M'Intosh, Charles, *The Book of the Garden*, ii (Edinburgh and London, 1855); M'Intosh, Charles, *The Flower Garden* (London, 1838); Mollison, John R., *The New Practical Window Gardener* (London, 1877); Moore, Thomas, *A Popular History of British Ferns* (London, 1862); Nicholson, George, *The Illustrated Dictionary of Gardening* (London, 1887); Robinson, William, *Alpine Flowers for English Gardens* (London, 1879); Robinson, William, *The English Flower Garden* (London, 1883); Robinson William, *The Wild Garden* (London, 1870); Rogers, W. S., *Villa Gardens* (London, 1902); Skill, Rebekah, *The Art of Modelling Wax Flowers* (London, 1852); Smee, Alfred, *My Garden: Its Plan and Culture* (London, 1872); Thompson, Robert, *The Gardener's Assistant: Practical and Scientific* (London, 1878); Thomson, David, *Handy Book of the Flower-Garden* (Edinburgh and London, 1868); Valentine, Mrs R. (ed.), *The Home Book of Pleasure and Instruction* (London, 1868); Warner, Charles Dudley, *My Summer in a Garden* (London, 1876); Wood, Samuel, *The Ladies' Multum-in-Parvo Flower Garden* (London, 1881); Ward, H. W., *My Gardener: A Practical Handbook for the Million* (London, 1891); *The Young Ladies' Journal Language of Flowers* (London, 1869). (The dates given are those of the editions consulted and not necessarily of first publication.)